MW01290268

FRANK

An independent, creative force in the astrological community for a quarter of a century, Frank Clifford has built an eclectic career in astrology, palmistry and publishing:

- as the writer of a dozen books, and columnist for numerous magazines
- as a publisher of over 30 books and booklets
- as a consultant for clients and businesses
- as a researcher and compiler of birth data
- as a media astrologer/palmist profiled and interviewed on radio, TV and in print
- as an international lecturer and the Principal of The London School of Astrology

In September 2012, at the annual Astrological Association Conference, Frank became the thirteenth (and youngest) winner of The Charles Harvey Award for Exceptional Service to Astrology – a lifetime achievement honour.

An astrologer and palmist since age 16, Frank began his data collecting work with Lois Rodden, contributing to and editing *Profiles of Women* (1995) and *Data News*. When Rodden was approached to develop software to house the data collection, Frank suggested she call it 'Astrodatabank'. His own Clifford Data Compendium first appeared as part of the Solar Fire package in 1997 (updated in 2000) and his first book, *British Entertainers: the Astrological Profiles*, was published that same year (expanded in 2003; new edition due 2017).

In 1996, Frank founded Flare Publications (www.flareuk.com), and since then has edited and published over two dozen astrology books. Frank's own books include *Getting to the Heart of Your Chart* (2012) and *Horoscope Snapshots* (2014). In recent years, he has focused on shorter volumes, including *Solar Arc Directions* (2011) and *The Midheaven: Spotlight on Success* (2015).

Frank has written Sun sign columns for magazines such as *Marie Claire* (UK), *Quick and Simple* (US), *Reveal* (UK) and *Candis* (UK). His media work has ranged from the sublime to the ridiculous: from documentaries on *Little Britain* and Danny Boyle's feature film *Sunshine* and working with the Oxford University Press and Universal Studios, to being asked by *The Sun* tabloid to locate a then-missing Saddam Hussein! Frank currently writes for *The Mountain Astrologer* and has guest edited half a dozen themed issues for the popular magazine.

Frank also has an international reputation as a palmist, with the *Guardian* dubbing him 'palm reader to the stars'. His palmistry books have been published in nine languages and his first, *Palmistry 4 Today* (Rider/Random House, 2002; Flare expanded edition, 2010), is considered the modern textbook on the subject.

Since Frank took over the running of The London School of Astrology in 2004, he has been instrumental in bringing a younger generation to the subject. He has also lectured in a dozen countries over four continents and given close to a thousand talks, classes and seminars. He was a guest tutor on a psychology course at the London Metropolitan University and, when Frank first visited China in 2012, the Press promoted him as 'the Dean of the Harry Potter School'! At the LSA he runs certificate and diploma classes, seminars and residential courses in astrology and palmistry. The LSA prides itself on inviting an eclectic range of some of the most accomplished astrologers from around the world to give seminars and classes. Online courses are due in 2017, as is a new textbook on interpretation and forecasting for students. For more details, visit www.londonschoolofastrology.co.uk and www.frankclifford.co.uk

To Barry Street, a most generous Sagittarian spirit

First edition published 2016 by Flare Publications and the London School of Astrology, BCM Planets, London WC1N 3XX, England, UK; Tel: 0700 2 33 44 55 www.flareuk.com and www.londonschoolofastrology.co.uk Email: info@flareuk.com A CIP catalogue record for this book is available from the British Library

Charts: Solar Fire software • Cover: Craig Knottenbelt • Proofing: Jane Struthers, Michael Nile

Thanks to Craig for the great cover, to Michael for the lifelong friendship and for his amazing Mercury–Saturn support during this project, and to the wonderful Jane and her Jupiter–MC in Virgo skills. Thanks to Bernard Eccles for clarifying (and simplifying!) the astronomy. And a big thank you to all the colleagues, friends, clients and students who have taught me so much and supported my work over the years.

I've been promising to produce a volume on the Midheaven for the longest time! I was on the point of sitting down to write it back in 2003 but then I began running The London School of Astrology, which became one of a handful of full-time jobs I've juggled for over ten years. The schedule shows no signs of abating, so the only way to finish this was to write a to-the-point booklet – to pack in as much as I possibly could and then leave further exploration of examples to future lectures and articles. It suits my Aries Sun and Gemini Ascendant, as well as my Virgo Moon. The reader response to the booklets already on the market has been heartening, so I hope you will enjoy this one, too. With my thanks and gratitude, Frank

Recent titles by Frank C. Clifford
The Astrology of Love, Sex & Attraction (2015); *Humour in the Horoscope: The Astrology of Comedy* (2015); *Horoscope Snapshots: Essays in Modern Astrology* (2014); *Getting to the Heart of Your Chart: Playing Astrological Detective* (2012); *Solar Arc Directions* (2011); *Palmistry 4 Today* (US Edition, 2010); *The Astrologer's Book of Charts* (2009)

The birth data of famous people listed in this booklet are from verified sources and full details can be found online at www.astrodatabank.com and Sy Scholfield's www.astrodatablog.com

Further reading on the Midheaven (listed alphabetically by author)
Planets in Work by Jamie Binder; *Power of the Midheaven* by Stephanie Jean Clement; *Vocation: the Astrology of Career, Creativity and Calling* by Brian Clark; *Using Astrology to Create a Vocational Profile* by Faye Cossar; *Vocational Astrology* by Judith Hill; *Aspects to Horoscope Angles* by Vivia Jayne; *Equal Houses* by Beth Koch; *Incarnation* by Melanie Reinhart; *Money: How to Find It with Astrology* by Lois Rodden; *Direction and Destiny in the Birthchart* by Howard Sasportas; *Finding Success in the Horoscope* by Jackie Slevin; *The Astrology of Success* by Jan Spiller; *Vocations* by Noel Tyl; *In Search of a Fulfilling Career* by Joanne Wickenburg

Introducing the Midheaven

When I first began to write, research and lecture on the Midheaven (Latin: *medium coeli* – pronounced *cheh-lee* – 'middle of the sky'), it was either generally overlooked in most astrological literature, included in descriptions of the 10th House or dismissed as simply a 'career' or non-personal point. It is, of course, much more than one's career. The Midheaven (or MC for short) describes facets of our public persona and our reputation, as well as the underlying psychological and parental issues that drive us to make our individual mark in the world. It is the area of the chart most associated with success, achievement and recognition, and is one of the four all-important angles of the horoscope – the most personal and time-sensitive points of our chart.

In this booklet, I'll be offering further definitions of the MC as well as looking at its role as part of an axis. I'll also offer some brief interpretations of the MC through the signs, its aspects from the planets and the various Ascendant–MC combinations (there are 38 possibilities for anyone born between the latitudes 60° North and 40° South).

If you know your birth time, you can use the graph on the next page to work out the sign of your Midheaven (or you can use a chart calculation program online). If your birth time is rounded off and/or your calculations show the MC degree to be close to the beginning or end of a sign, I hope the descriptions in this booklet will help you determine in which sign your MC actually falls.

But first, a little astronomy. Your Midheaven is the degree of the ecliptic (the apparent path of the Sun) that is due south at the moment and place of your birth (for southern hemisphere births, the MC is due north). The MC degree is exactly opposite the Imum Coeli ('bottom of the sky', or IC for short) – they are the same degree and minute, but in signs opposite one another.

Whereas the time it takes for the Ascendant degree to rise can vary (in the northern hemisphere, Virgo, Libra and Scorpio rise particularly slowly and Pisces, Aries and Taurus rise quickly – and these are reversed in the southern hemisphere), the Midheaven is like clockwork. It takes four minutes to move 1° through the zodiac, taking a full two hours to travel through a sign (each sign comprises 30°; 4 mins x 30 = 2 hours).

On page 18 of this booklet, when writing about the Equal system of house division (where each house is 30°, starting from the Ascendant's degree), I shall introduce the zenith (the degree of the zodiac directly above the observer) and the nadir (the degree directly underneath the observer) – both are 90° from the Ascendant–Descendant axis.

The Power Points of the Horoscope: The Four Angles

Before we focus on the Midheaven, it is worthwhile seeing it in the context of the other horoscope angles. The angles of our chart are not celestial bodies but four important astronomical reference points at the moment of our birth. As four 'anchors', 'pillars', 'hinges' or 'compass points' (renowned astrologer William Lilly called them 'the quarters of heaven'), they provide a framework for the horoscope and determine the twelve astrological houses, which then bring the planets 'down to earth' and blend the celestial of the 'above' with the mundane of the 'below'. The four angles are, in fact, two axes: the Ascendant–Descendant axis and the MC–IC axis. Axes are oppositions: the sign on the Ascendant is exactly opposite that of the Descendant, and the MC opposes the IC. The nature of oppositions is to make us conscious of both inseparable

Calculating Your MC • Position a ruler vertically from your birth date (top row) downwards to align with your birth time (bottom row), having first deducted any summer/daylight savings time (usually 1 hour). The section of the strip it passes through (middle row) is your MC sign. Look to see whether it's in the first, middle or final ten degrees (decan – page 23) of the sign, too.

Date

Key to Zodiac Glyphs:

♈ Aries
♉ Taurus
♊ Gemini

♋ Cancer
♌ Leo
♍ Virgo

♎ Libra
♏ Scorpio
♐ Sagittarius

♑ Capricorn
♒ Aquarius
♓ Pisces

Midheaven

Local Sidereal Time

Local Mean Time

Larger, laminated versions of this nomogram and the ascendant calculator are available from:
The Astrology Shop, Covent Garden, London: www.londonastrology.com
Design copyright © Mick Soar: www.llun.net

and interlinked ends – and how an emphasis on one can affect the other. The Ascendant and Midheaven are usually considered the most important 'directions' of the four angles, and arrowheads are usually added to these lines in a chart (see below).

Planets **'manifest' most decisively and powerfully** at the four angles; here the planets make their mark as **recurring themes, character traits, relationship patterns and life scripts**. Whether we're practising natal (birth), electional, forecasting or horary astrology, a planet within 8–10° of an angle makes the most obvious set of statements about the person or situation. Natally, a planet on an angle shows **that which is called forth for us to enact and fulfil most vividly in our lifetime**. In *Getting to the Heart of Your Chart* (Flare, 2012), I wrote, 'The four angles … act like a **highly personal compass**: they reveal **our orientation to our environment**; and they are also 'receivers', showing what we pick up from our surroundings and how we interact with the world around us. They are **two-way windows on our world**, representing our personal [Ascendant], relationship [Descendant], family [IC] and social landscapes [MC].'

Most systems of house division are quadrant-based: each of the four angles begins a quadrant (see diagram) and an angular house. Although I don't use a quadrant house system, each angle could be symbolically assigned an element (and cardinal sign) that corresponds to the 'natural' sign order anticlockwise from the Ascendant:

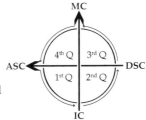

- ❖ The Ascendant (ASC) begins the 1st Quadrant and the 1st House, which is linked to the **Fire** sign of **Aries** and ruler Mars.
- ❖ The Imum Coeli (IC) begins the 2nd Quadrant and the 4th House, which is linked to the **Water** sign of **Cancer** and ruler Moon.
- ❖ The Descendant (DSC) begins the 3rd Quadrant and the 7th House, which is linked to the **Air** sign of **Libra** and ruler Venus.
- ❖ The Medium Coeli (MC) begins the 4th Quadrant and the 10th House, which is linked to the **Earth** sign of **Capricorn** and ruler Saturn.

These associations help us to define each angle and capture their differences:

- ❖ **The Ascendant** (Fire angle): What motivates me as I walk out my front door and face the world. How I interpret experience and engage with life. How I expect the world to appear, and how I appear (including my physicality) to it. The choices I make based upon expectations and experience. My own idea of reality and my open agenda. The route and journey/myth through life. My meet-and-greet personality. *My identity badge.*
- ❖ **The IC** (Water angle): My foundations, legacy, ancestors, heritage, roots and 'soil'; my psychological taproot. My 'cellar'; who I am when alone, germinating, feeling lonely or when I retreat. My deep subconscious. Hidden motivations to succeed in the outer world. The area of my life I ignore at my peril; secret fears that can unconsciously steer my direction. Any founding principles I have that anchor a sense of security (i.e. what I *know* belongs to me). *My family coat of arms.*
- ❖ **The Descendant** (Air angle): My own reflection/projection through my relationships with friends and lovers. What I need to receive from others (even

when not aware of it). Others' perceptions of me and interactions that challenge the notion of who I am and force me to consider how I come across to the world. What I attract and seek out in a partner. *My personals ad.*

❖ **The MC** (Earth angle): My aims and goals, and intentions (inner 'vow') to create something of substance and lasting impact for the world to see. My place of mastery and distinction. My best pathway to social recognition; me at my most conscious. What I stand for in the world. *My resumé or professional ID.*

As I wrote in *Heart*, the Ascendant–Descendant axis is like a see-saw – the challenge is the balancing act of 'I' and 'you' – negotiating, compromising, seeking equality and equilibrium. This axis is our horizon – the direction is left and right, east and west – what we see when we scan our surroundings; what grabs our attention. It is **the axis of encounters** – engaging with our environment, interacting with people around us, and our relationship issues.

The MC–IC axis is like a vertical pillar or tree – how we are able to grow up and out. In order to soar (MC), we must be aware of the ground below us (IC) and the steadiness of our foundation. A 'spinal column' or backbone, this is the **axis of individuality, hierarchy, parents and self-actualization.** The challenge is the balancing act of becoming our own construct in society without putting our principles and past completely in the shade. The direction of this axis is above and below, so it asks us to look up towards the (middle of the) heavens, out of ourselves and into the future, as well as to look down, deep inside and back to our roots.

As mentioned, the angles reveal the orientation of our personal compass to our environment, which may or may not immediately blend well with key horoscope placements such as the Sun and Moon and the inner planets. Perhaps all four angles are in **fixed** signs (suggesting a permanent environment and attachment to it) or **cardinal** (a dynamic environment that requires initiating and engaging in life's central conflicts) or **mutable** signs (a changeable environment with shifting goalposts) – or a mix of different modes. If we have fixed signs on our angles but inner planets (from the Sun to Mars) that have an emphasis on mutable signs, the fixed environment might feel frustrating or restrictive to our mutable nature – or it might provide much-needed stability and give others the impression that we are more stable and grounded (fixed angles) than we naturally are (mutable inner planets). If we have a mutable compass, though, the environment might be one of constant process and change that suits a flexible temperament (mutable inner planets) – or it might unsteady those of us with fixed inner planets who need stability and predictability.

The Work of the Gauquelins

From the 1950s to the 1980s, French statisticians Michel and Françoise Gauquelin found that any attempt to 'prove' astrology hinged on the angles. They proved that planets around the four angles determined facets of our character as well as eminence in certain professions. Using a Placidus-type system of house division, they showed that **the areas around the angles were the most powerful, character-defining positions in the chart.** But to the dismay of many astrologers, the findings leaned towards the cadent houses (12th, 9th, 6th and

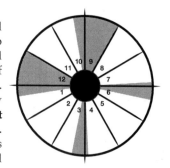

3rd) of the horoscope rather than the anticipated neighbouring angular 1st, 4th, 7th and 10th houses – for so long considered the most important areas. At birth, a planet in any of the four Gauquelin Sectors (or G-Zones) – see the shaded areas of the diagram above – has a powerful bearing on **our most fundamental, innate and compelling drives**. It makes a strong, lifelong impression on us.

The Gauquelins attained results with the Moon, Venus, Mars, Jupiter and Saturn (perhaps the Sun and Mercury's closeness in the sky obscured any noticeable patterns for either planet), and when I was last with Françoise, many years ago, she spoke of 'getting results' with Uranus. Although most of the Gauquelins' work examined the links between eminent professionals and associated planets (e.g. leading, top brass athletes had Mars in a G-Zone more often than expected and more than regular athletes), their greatest legacy to astrologers is their keyword research into the planets. They were able to compile lists of adjectives that created 'planetary types' (e.g. the Mars type is 'spontaneous', 'fearless', 'combative', 'dynamic', 'energetic' and 'reckless'). This took their research away from 'eminence' (which is not particularly useful in everyday astrological consultations) to that of building a 'nature' for each planet – a collection of characteristics that produces resonant effects in every area of a person's life.

The Diurnal Cycle

The planets (unless retrograde) move anticlockwise through the zodiac. But on a daily (diurnal) cycle, the Earth's rotation on its axis means that planets appear to move clockwise: to rise over the Ascendant and culminate at the MC, then set at the Descendant and anti-culminate at the IC (see the arrows around the diagram, right). The Ascendant–Descendant 'horizon' axis is the distinction between light and dark: that which is potentially visible to the observer (above the horizon, houses 12 to 7) and that which is hidden (below the horizon, houses 1 to 6).

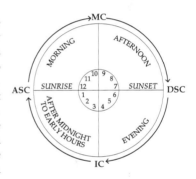

The Sun is the great cosmic clock; its position in a horoscope will give you an immediate idea as to the time a person was born. Here's what I wrote for *The Contemporary Astrologer's Handbook* (Flare, 2006): 'The Sun rises from the First Quadrant and crosses the Ascendant (sunrise), moving above the horizon into the Fourth Quadrant (**morning**). It passes across the MC (around noon) and into the Third Quadrant after midday (**afternoon**), and then heads down towards the horizon (Descendant). After crossing the horizon/Descendant (around sunset), it travels down into the Second Quadrant (**evening**). By midnight (Sun on the IC) it is ready to move from the Second to the First Quadrant (where it travels from the lowest part of the horoscope – **early hours** – up towards the horizon and a new sunrise).' (Keep in mind of course that sunrise and sunset vary depending on the time of year and how far north or south we are. In the UK, for instance, during the summer months we have Daylight Savings Time, so clocks register GMT noon and midnight at 1 p.m. and 1 a.m. respectively.)

We can take the Sun's path through the day and night as a good analogy of the four angles. The IC point is the eerie, midnight 'low' point – the crossover from one day to the next. At this point, all is dark, unconscious, quiet, internal. And then some hours later, the new 'day' begins at sunrise as the Sun crosses over the Ascendant and into the 12th House. It's a birth, an emergence. It's a spectacular, unmissable launch. (*Keywords: emergence, ascension, ascendancy, magnification, burgeoning.*) We then reach the glaring light of 'high noon' at the Midheaven (MC) – the Sun's peak position, its glorious culmination. (*Keywords: pedestal, splendour, bloom, eminence, pinnacle, apex, culmination, climax, high point.*) The Sun glides down towards the Descendant and 'dies' as it merges with the horizon and 'loses itself' at sunset. (*Keywords: merging, uniting, integration, bowing, curtain call, demise, disappearance, sinking, withdrawal, fade.*) It then heads down towards the midnight position of the IC again, finishing the 24-hour cycle. (*Keywords: retreat, conversion, changeover, transition, depth, low point.*) The Sun is at its most impressive at three of the angles and significantly invisible to us at the IC. (Astrologer Melanie Reinhart quips that the IC should be known as the 'I don't see' because of its hidden nature.)

Although I've used the Sun as an example, during the course of 24 hours each planet crosses over these important astronomical positions and follows a similar path of dark crossover (anti-culminating at the IC), emergence (rising at the ASC), culmination (peaking at the MC) and disappearance (setting at the DSC). (Due to the Earth's rotation, every degree of the zodiac will appear on each angle at some point during 24 hours as the Earth turns on its axis and we get a 360° view of the heavens in that time.)

This clockwise, diurnal movement of the planets is different from the sequence of the houses, which are counted in an anticlockwise manner from the Ascendant (see diagram, right). Once the birth moment has occurred, an Ascendant (and its degree) can be calculated, and the houses then follow on from this Ascendant/rising sign. The signs of the zodiac follow this sequence, too, as do planets when they transit the natal horoscope.

There have been a number of interesting methods (from astrologers such as Dorotheus, Guido Bonatti and William Lilly to Wolfgang Döbereiner, Tad Mann and Bruno and Louise Huber) to align these angles and quadrants with stages or years of life. Although some astrologers use the anticlockwise, regular order of the houses to determine the age or stage in life, I think the clockwise, diurnal movement is equally revealing:

❖ At the IC, a planet is at its starting and earliest point (like a New Moon). A planet travelling up towards the Ascendant is incubating, developing; it's in the dark, in the seeding stage. The planet hasn't yet come to light. Symbolically this is the **conception point** (IC), which is followed by the **gestating stage in the womb**.

❖ At the Ascendant, a planet crosses over and emerges into the light – it is visible, active and striving (like the First Quarter Moon). As it journeys through what we know to be the 12th House and up to the MC, it is early and unaware – but we slowly witness the awareness and conscious development of this young energy. It is striving, on its way and heading towards the top. Symbolically it is the moment from **birth** (the Ascendant) **up until the first Saturn return or perhaps the mid-30s**. When it reaches its highest point of the journey, the planet is at the Midheaven (MC) – at its peak energy-wise and in full glory. It has reached maturity, like the Full Moon.

❖ The planet begins to travel down towards the Descendant. Symbolically it is the period between the **first and second Saturn returns** (29–59). At the Descendant (like the Last Quarter Moon), it begins to disappear, actively changing gear, submerging into 'old age', the twilight years and the final act in life.

❖ The planet is now below the surface – hidden – as it heads towards the 'bottom of the sky', the IC. Symbolically this is the period from **retirement to death**. Once it has passed the IC point, a planet is 're-seeded', gestates and starts its climb towards its re-emergence (birth) at the Ascendant. Like a foetus ready to emerge into the world, a planet about to rise from the 1st House into the 12th is equipped with just enough of what it needs for its launch into the light (even if it is at a vulnerable, early stage).

Ancient star-watchers considered the Descendant to be the point of death – opposite the Ascendant, the point of birth – when the Sun or planet would disappear from sight and travel below the horizon; but in our diurnal, clockwise method, the IC is the switchover, the death point, the 'end of the matter'.

It's not a complete stretch to combine both directions in your approach: to use the anticlockwise 1–12 Equal houses (or another house system) for the house meanings in natal and forecasting work (to show the mundane, psychological and archetypal experiences in action); and also to use the quadrants in a diurnal, clockwise manner (to describe a natal planet's place in the cycle/ages/seasons of life). (Astrologer Glenda Cole took a different route and wrote a fascinating article looking at how the house meanings could be explained by starting from the 12th all the way around to the 1st, as the Gauquelins also suggested.)

The Midheaven (MC): What it Means in Our Horoscope

Ideally, the MC should not be read in isolation – for a full understanding of its meaning, we must consider the rest of the chart. It is also a complex unto itself: we cannot look at the MC sign without looking at both ends of the axis, its planetary ruler(s), aspects from the planets and, if we choose a non-quadrant system, to look at the house in which it falls. Here's a summary, which is followed by a guide to what the MC means.

❖ Our definitions of success; how we receive social recognition
❖ Our status, image and reputation
❖ Qualities we admire, elevate and emulate; our role models
❖ Our social shorthand; the public perception of our lifestyle
❖ Our game plan; where we're heading
❖ Early aspirations
❖ Parental themes; our parental inheritance

The Formula for Success: Grabbing the Brass Ring

Success is shown in a chart by the extent to which we assume the role symbolized by the MC voluntarily and constructively – Lois Rodden, *Money: How to Find It with Astrology* (Data New Press, 1995)

Success is symbolized in the horoscope by the Midheaven (MC). Success is: 'the attainment of a goal and recognition for it; a favourable outcome of something attempted; the attainment of wealth, position, honours.' The etymology of the word lies in *succedere* (to come after, to ascend, to mount) and *successus* (an advance, a coming up; a good result), and both corroborate the MC's astronomical position as an elevated point in the horoscope close to where planets culminate (*culminatus*: to top, to crown) and reach their peak.

The MC sign (as well its aspects from the planets) spotlights **the sort of success that gives us personal fulfilment**, as well as those **aims that we define as success** (be they money, stability, family, love, fame, etc). And in turn, what we would consider failure – what we'd significantly miss if we weren't able to achieve it. Ideally the MC is **a place of triumph**; where we are crowned for our achievements.

When we look at our Midheaven sign – and particularly any planets conjunct the MC – it gives us an idea of **the images or tableaux we have around achievement:** winning an award, being CEO of a company, having a book published, becoming a millionaire, receiving standing ovations, gathering together with our loving family, making the world a better place, etc. Nowadays people associate success with money and fame, and to read some astrological texts on the subject we imagine all we'd need was the Sun in the 10th House or Jupiter on the Midheaven to be famous. But whereas the MC *does* speak of our type of 'fame' and our most notable achievements, a planet on the MC (or in the 10th House) does not guarantee any measure of success or fame – neither does a weakly or 'badly' aspected MC (or ruler) suggest the opposite. The more charts we read, the more we realize that there is no simple formula. People become successful or 'famous' (locally, nationally or globally) for as many reasons and in as many ways as there are planetary combinations and astrological indicators to describe them. The chart says far more about our motivation, talents and our approach to any field of endeavour than it does about what 'makes' a successful astrologer, politician, teacher or famous person.

Most of us will work without a moment of fame (or interest in it, perhaps), but it is important for us all to have some measure of acclaim for our contribution to the world around us. Ultimately, I think the keys to any sort of success are the three Ds: Discipline, Determination and Drive. In short: Courage. We all have some kind of talent and a level of energy to accomplish tasks, but without courage we can't truly express our potential. Here's a formula I've written before in my books: **Talent + Energy + Courage = Success in Life.**

Back to the Midheaven. Whether we're aiming for the world stage or to make an impact on our local, social environment, this angle shows **the best pathway to success and outer recognition**. Unlike the Moon, which speaks of primal needs and habits formed in childhood, the MC takes time (the Saturn, Earth angle) to formulate, build and to bloom. The MC acts as a gateway, a portal to 'out there', beyond ourselves. Its sign and whole complex reveals **the types of behaviour and image we need to cultivate in order to receive acknowledgement from others and form a successful reputation in society**. The MC–IC axis also warns of the types of conduct that can get in the way of our own successes, ruin our reputation or thwart our accomplishments.

This guide to 'best behaviour' (as shown by the MC and its aspects) may be in conflict or in harmony with our temperament (as shown by the Moon) or our personal philosophy and core life direction (as symbolized by the Sun). And our horoscope will reveal whether other chart factors clash with or support the message of the MC complex. Lois Rodden writes in *Money*: 'The extent of the contradiction between the MC and our basic nature shows the extent of distress or inability to function in a successful societal role.' But no combination 'denies' success – in fact, contradictions can spur us on, or we will find that 'hard' discordant aspects to the MC mirror the determination and backbone we have that helps us succeed. But some combinations work together more easily and then we start to see the 'triumvirate' between the Moon (needs), Sun (core character) and MC (societal conduct) complementing each other. We'll be looking at a few examples later.

Yes, S.I.R.! Status, Image, Reputation

What one has to do usually can be done – Eleanor Roosevelt

The MC is linked to our **status** – our social or work position, **our professional standing**, our station in life. These come with certain rights, obligations and responsibilities. Do we need (or command) respect? How do we appear when we're 'on show'? Astrologer Jackie Slevin calls the Midheaven our 'personal marketplace' and 'our state of public presentation'. Being linked to Saturn, Capricorn and the 10th House, the MC speaks of **our relationship with authority and hierarchy**. Although planets residing in the 10th can clearly describe our authority figures and bosses, the MC has much to say about **how we assume our own authority in the world**, and our approach to 'the system'.

How willing are we to fit into a societal role and handle **our reputation, responsibilities and expectations** (as well as those of others)? This all requires energy and striving. In some ways, we must prove our Midheaven complex to the world in order to earn our place in it and to be of genuine service.

What do we stand for? Our vision of what we want for ourselves is tested at the Midheaven. Astrologer Michael Munkasey warns, 'If you feel you have a meaningless role in life, then the fault lies with you, not with your 10th House or astrology. Accomplishment and recognition in life are given for work done, not work promised.' It is a sign of maturity when we discover that we must work within certain constraints, rules and laws (Saturn) and cannot have everything handed to us without question.

Success is not the key to happiness. Happiness is the key to success.
If you love what you are doing, you will be successful – Albert Schweitzer

Success is getting what you want; happiness is wanting what you get – Dale Carnegie

Our public image can take years to build and, like the true message of the Sun in our chart, it can take a long time to truly recognize the meaning of our Midheaven. Earning our position over the years is the best way to comfortably 'grow into' our MC complex and master the qualities it represents. Identifying – and then feeling comfortable with – **our mission** and our trajectory is essential to avoid comparison and unnecessary expectation (recipes for unhappiness in our relationships with ourselves and others). But if we assume the role of the MC too soon or create a false or surface image, we may feel like an impostor, waiting to be told we don't belong. Inevitably 'life' conspires to show others what we fear most: we get 'found out' as a fake.

The Midheaven's sign symbolizes something that we spontaneously flow toward and grow toward as we get older (although we may exhibit some of those qualities in 'seed form' while we are young), but it does often require effort to attain the optimum expression of those qualities
– Stephen Arroyo, *Astrology, Karma & Transformation* (CRCS, 1978)

We can, as Arroyo suggests, 'spontaneously' gravitate towards the characteristics of our MC sign, but the key is *active participation*: being aware of the various levels of the sign, and cultivating behaviour that reflects our highest aspirations and the greatest parts of ourselves. The MC is the area of the chart most linked to **self-actualization in the outside world**. The MC shows the direction our life takes when we move into society. But as astrologer Steven Forrest (in *The Inner Sky*, ACS, 1988) writes: 'Navigating the Midheaven is never easy ... Before it can blossom, we must first know ourselves very well. We must have sorted out our destiny from all that "doctor, lawyer, Indian chief" programming we received while growing up. If we succeed, we are at home in the world. Our work, our status, our public identity – all reflect what is going on inside us.'

So we must embrace the qualities of our MC. A true understanding of **our social identity – our personal role in public** – leads to an inner sense of authority, integrity and balance; we know who we are to other people and have a good idea of our status in our community and role in the world. We can attain, accomplish and receive rewards with an open heart when we're at home with our MC complex. Life flows. Things click. As a result of our efforts, opportunities arise that are in harmony with our true self and the life awaiting us. I am reminded of Joseph Campbell's advice to 'follow our bliss'.

The Public Angles: The Midheaven and Ascendant

Together, the Ascendant and Midheaven angles form discrete parts of **our image and public persona**, components of our distinctive identity and our contract with society. The Ascendant is our persona (designed for face-to-face interaction), while the MC is our reputation (built for self-actualization and a place in the community). Both are social roles with two-way impacts: we take steps to construct these aspects of ourselves – to make an impression on the world around us – and in turn others evaluate and form opinions based on these impressions (and their own set of motivations, expectations and viewpoints). These angles are **vehicles** on our journey; we use them to steer the planets in our chart. The angles are the framework but the planets are the core components of our multifaceted natures. Later, I'll introduce the Ascendant signs possible with each Midheaven placement and write key phrases on each.

The Hero at High Noon

The MC complex tells us about **the qualities we admire in others** and **how we attempt to emulate these qualities**. Which personal characteristics impress us? Do we admire strength, risk-taking, versatility? Are we swayed by initiative, perseverance, integrity, independence? **Which traits would we prefer *to be seen* to possess?** For what would we like to be **held in esteem**? Would we like to be known as a carer, a free spirit, a hard worker, an original?

The MC is something we look up to like the top of a cathedral spire or a ship's mast. It is the peak above, an uppermost limit, and a symbol of something worth reaching for – Brian Clark, 'Getting an Angle on the Axes of the Horoscope', *The Mountain Astrologer*, June–July 2013

In the horoscope, the Sun is the image of the hero (and the hero within), but the MC is the 'high noon' position where **the hero flourishes 'out there' and shines at his or her brightest**. It is our appointment with destiny, a time of potency and creative splendour. The MC is a public point – a place where we announce ourselves and **declare our intentions**. (It is interesting to note how many weddings take place when couples have transits, progressions or directions involving their MC placements, and that inaugurations and royal coronations are traditionally timed for noon, when the Sun is on or near the Midheaven.) In *Astrology for the Light Side of the Brain* (ACS, 1995), Kim Rogers-Gallagher calls the MC our own 'personal bulletin board … where you put all your accomplishments and all the things you want the world to know about you.'

The MC blends our aspirations with **our inspirations**: **our role models** – the people and things we grew up admiring, **elevating** and putting on a pedestal, and **the people, traits and situations we respect as adults**. Working out specifically what we admire about a person can take a bit of digging. For instance, if we admire the singer **TINA TURNER**, do we applaud her vocal talents, her dynamic energy, her sensuality, her survival story of spousal abuse, or her Buddhist beliefs – or a mix of these? Fan worship or sexual attraction aside, there will usually be a deeper thread that connects the lives and characteristics of the various people we admire. Often we esteem those whose Sun, Ascendant or MC placements connect in some way with our own (usually by sign and within a 5° conjunction). Those things above that Turner is known for can be found in the mix of her Sun in Sagittarius, Ascendant in Leo and MC in Taurus.

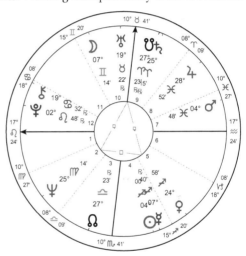

How we look from a social distance … how we look to people who do not know us. What do they see? They see what we symbolize to them … as embodiments of various functions in society – Steven Forrest, *The Inner Sky* (ACS, 1988)

When consulting, I usually begin a session with a new client by describing their MC sign (and planets conjunct) because this often describes how we get pigeonholed (Saturn has links to categorizing and typecasting) and **how others label us before they truly know us** (or based on what they hear about us from others). Discussing the MC before I address more intimate parts of the client's chart acts as an icebreaker and can be articulated with a certain detachment. (Interestingly, it's also often what they're keen to show off about themselves when they book the appointment or arrive at my door.) It is much more helpful to describe a client's Midheaven than to go straight to their Moon placement, which is often an Achilles heel and can prompt them to clam up. It's not that the MC isn't an intimate component of who we are, but that it's **the easiest part of ourselves to externalize** – for us to see with some objectivity – and is often **the most obvious thing about our reputation,** or **the phrases others use to introduce or describe us.**

A reputation can be met with a grudging acceptance: being in the public eye means we might have to share all sorts of dirty laundry that otherwise wouldn't go further than the gossips in the local community centre. Take a look at the horoscope of **BORIS BECKER,** who has Uranus and Venus either side of his Midheaven in Libra. In zodiac sequence, Uranus is first up, suggesting his overnight success on the tennis circuit as a prodigy – he won Wimbledon *out of the blue* (Uranus) as an unseeded 17-year-old in 1985. Later, Venus and the Libra MC came into play as he was known for his sex life ('Bonking Boris'), his investment in a fashion line of clothing and his interracial marriage (which provoked much hostility from bigots) – plus the extramarital quickie he had in a Japanese restaurant in London, which was much publicised and produced a daughter.

Soundbite Summaries

The first adages I recall hearing about the MC were that it describes **a destiny point, how we'd like to be remembered, what we want on our tombstone** and **the first line of our obituary.** In short: the mark we'd like to make on our world, **our legacy.** The MC is both the road taken towards achievement and the actual arrival: **the direction and destination.**

As an astrological symbol of our reputation, the MC can act as our **social shorthand** – how we describe what we do in life and for work. When someone asks, 'What do you do for a living?', we may tell them our job title ('systems analyst', 'environmental maintenance officer'), but this says more about the PC climate we live in than what we actually *do.* It may sound pretentious to answer 'eternal student' or 'people person', but in essence the MC complex reveals precisely those types of things.

Missions and Motivations

> *The career point par excellence … a mission statement for life. One's material accomplishments and professional aspirations are represented [at the MC]. It can also indicate outer events that seem to control the life externally, from above as it were. –* Judith Hill, *Vocational Astrology* (AFA, 2000)

I like to work with clients and students on their MC complex to form a **mission statement.** One of the best ways to start is by looking at the element of our MC sign. **The element shows what motivates, stimulates and inspires us to be a part of society and to succeed in our endeavours;** what spurs us on towards goals; our incentive.

A Fire Midheaven (Aries, Leo, Sagittarius) ignites in fields offering challenge, competition, excitement and risk. Those of us with a fiery MC seek glory, greatness and recognition of our individuality rather than money or position; we wish to enthuse others and are fuelled by passion and optimism. We are hustlers, (self-)promoters, evangelists, visionaries, inspirational teachers, life coaches and leaders.

Those of us with a Midheaven in an Earth sign (Taurus, Virgo, Capricorn) wish to find a role in the world that provides security and to engage with work that is expedient and delivers tangible results. We wish to leave the world a better place than we found it. We seek routine and a steady income and prefer to stay with the known and familiar. Gaining pleasure from a job well done, we aim to be reliable providers, dependable 'rocks' and productive, purposeful 'realists'. We are the craftsmen, builders (of anything, from homes to empires), lovers and supporters of our countryside. We are sensualists and work directly with our bodies (e.g. sport, massage or gardening).

Those of us with an Air Midheaven (Gemini, Libra, Aquarius) come alive in fields offering exchange, dialogue and debate. We seek roles that provide variety, interaction and travel. We want to be seen as people who learn about the world and question life. We are interested in theory, concept, the abstract, formulas and patterns. At work, we aim to analyse, deduce and reason. We are known for our fascination with people and we make natural communicators, salespeople, persuaders and advocates.

With a Water Midheaven (Cancer, Scorpio, Pisces), we seek out areas of work and society that offer emotional bonds. We focus on human values and aim to be of service to the human condition. We focus on that which has not been verbalized and connect to that which cannot be articulated. We want to be seen as empathetic and sympathetic. Our antennae scan atmospheres for nuance and we are known for our spot-on judgements and vindicated gut instincts. We are the carers, counsellors, therapists and intuitives.

Another way to break down the signs into groups is to look at the MC's mode, which describes **our modus operandi in society, our way of negotiating conflict and how we navigate life's key areas**. Cardinal Midheavens (Aries, Cancer, Libra, Capricorn) are those of us who seek to be seen as self-determining individuals who enjoy assuming a leadership role, initiating projects and taking on challenges. With a fixed Midheaven (Taurus, Leo, Scorpio, Aquarius), we attach ourselves to principles, build on these and establish a position of power and purpose. If we have a mutable Midheaven (Gemini, Virgo, Sagittarius, Pisces), we favour the freedom to choose multiple paths and changeable lifestyles, which are usually linked to learning, communication, analysis and travel.

The MC can also be described as **our game plan** – a strategy for achieving goals and blossoming in society. As Lois Rodden reminds us in her excellent book *Money*, 'A clearly defined goal *which is realistically accessible* within a specific time window is the most appropriate method to attain a desired outcome.' Lois was born with Mercury opposite practical Saturn, which she rectified and placed on a Sagittarius Midheaven. Another pragmatic astrologer, Faye Cossar (Taurus MC), works with clients over a series of sessions to create a brand profile ('a set of characteristics or keywords that we can refer to as a checklist for … designing a leaflet, writing a bio or setting up a website'). Her chapter in *Using Astrology to Create a Vocational Profile* (Flare, 2012) entitled 'Expressing an Authentic Image' shows how to blend the qualities of our Sun placement (where our heart lies) with the Ascendant (how we come across) and MC (our mission, goals and reputation) signs. This creates a profile that can help with defining mission statements and work descriptions, and with finding logos and colours for personal and professional branding. These exercises are good ways of reminding us that we need to understand who we are, what we love and what we can offer. We can then find work that genuinely reflects who we are as an individual.

If we happen to be in the public eye, the MC complex can reveal **the public's perception of our lifestyle**. (Even if we don't have a high-profile job, it's still the impression that our social group has of us.) This is not just our image but also people's understanding of **how we navigate through life**. Is this with charm (Venus/Libra), assertion (Mars/Aries) or perspicacity (Mars/Scorpio)? In *Horoscope Snapshots* (Flare, 2014), I wrote that actors personify characters who are **vivid stereotypes and archetypes of the sign on those actors' Midheavens** (and, to a lesser extent, their Sun signs). The whole chart provides insight into the type of roles they play, but the MC is often **their most instantly recognized character**. Consider two actors whose most memorable roles are as James Bond. Sean Connery (Scorpio MC) played Bond as a dangerous, manly, sexual charismatic spy who treated his women with a touch of sadistic cruelty. Roger Moore (Taurus MC, plus Sun in Libra) played Bond as a smooth, debonair lover (more than a fighter) who could always be quietly and dryly amused by the antics of his opponents.

In *Snapshots*, I profiled actors who run the gamut of Scorpio on the MC: from Dustin Hoffman with his meticulous approach and intense portrayals, and Anthony Hopkins, most famous as the demonic cannibal in *Silence of the Lambs*, to *Bourne* and *Mr Ripley* star Matt Damon, Larry Hagman (the ruthless J.R. 'trust me' Ewing in *Dallas*), Val Kilmer, Robbie Coltrane (criminal psychologist *Cracker*), Maggie Kirkpatrick (famous as the sadistic warden in *Prisoner*) and 24 star Kiefer Sutherland. This list also included actresses who have shed a stereotypical Scorpio sex symbol image to play psychological or transformative roles, or taken up political causes away from the camera (Catherine Deneuve, Jane Fonda, Susan Sarandon).

MC–IC: The Parental Axis

Like the spinal column, the MC–IC supports the whole horoscope. At its base is the IC, which is rooted in the instinctual self and the familial gene pool; at the top is the MC, opening out onto the world at large. From earliest times, this was the parental axis, the mythological pair of opposites that support, foster, shape and socialize the self in the world – Brian Clark, 'Getting an Angle on the Axes of the Horoscope', *The Mountain Astrologer*, June–July 2013

As part of an axis with the IC, the MC can help us to define both **where we've come from** and **where we're heading** in life. (There are other interlinked points in the chart – the Moon and Sun, and the South and North Nodes – that relate to various levels of this journey.) Earlier I used the popular analogy of a tree, with the IC as the roots and soil and the MC as the branches and foliage. Another way to look at it is to see the MC as a skylight to which we look up for inspiration and receive illumination, and the IC is the basement laden with artefacts from our past and damp with memory.

As with the South Node to the North Node and the Moon to the Sun, we are required to muster the courage to leave the safety of our IC, risk the fears described by its sign placement (and planets nearby), and invest energy in making an impact on the world around us in the way described by our MC sign (and any planets conjunct it). Very often, with the MC–IC axis, **we want what we know (IC) until we know what we want (MC)**. But we can't know where we're going (MC) unless we know where we've been (IC). The MC is a call to leave the comfort zone and 'family name' of the IC and branch out on our own; to dare to carve our own name and reputation. The MC is the route 'up' – from our inner, private world (IC) – and out into the world.

But it is important not to abandon the IC entirely – not to leave our past in the shade and forget where we came from, what influenced us and what fuels us *deep inside*. With any axis in the chart, it's easy for us to stay at one end (angle) at the expense of the other. It's often the IC that gets neglected, and when that happens it can truly get in the way of our MC's progress and our feeling of accomplishment. The IC is both the womb and the tomb – a place where we can stay and feel fed and nurtured or restricted and entrapped. In order to make the best of this axis, we need to heed the words of George Santayana: 'Those who cannot remember the past are condemned to repeat it.'

The IC is **the subconscious motivation to achieve in the outside world**. It's important to identify the root causes (IC) of certain desires and shine a light onto our IC complex. For instance, a motivation to take centre stage and grab the attention (Leo on the IC), if gone unrecognized, can 'spoil' the fruits of working successfully for our community (Aquarius on the MC).

Sometimes a planet on the IC acts as an anchor, supporting its message by providing a sturdy foundation. A planet can feed the soil represented by the IC and help us to develop strong roots (IC), which in turn produce strong branches through the MC. But a planet on the IC can also act as a millstone or shackle when it becomes the excuse for us not flourishing or making courageous decisions in life (e.g. 'My parents held me back' – Saturn on the IC). Ultimately, it is truly our choice whether the IC sustains us or keeps us from branching out and blossoming. As my astrologer friend Jane de Rome says, 'We must feed the roots to taste the fruits.'

The IC complex shows **areas of life that we ignore at our peril**. These will present us with secret fears that unconsciously steer us. 'What lies beneath' has the power to control where we're going and to block those alternative paths that facilitate growth. It's the most hidden part of the chart and we must shine a light on it, explore its depths and see the part it plays in the development of our public role. For instance, in the chart of grocer's daughter turned UK Prime Minister Margaret Thatcher, Virgo is on the MC and Pisces on the IC. Engaging in work, getting a trade, earning a living, being self-sufficient and *doing something productive and useful* (Virgo MC) all played key roles in her policies, but she ignored (or had little patience for) the disenfranchised, unemployed and those unable to work (Pisces on the IC). So much of her legacy rests upon the Virgo–Pisces polarity and the vast disparity between the wealth made in the workplace by the few (upwardly-mobile entrepreneurs) and the poverty inflicted on the working class, whose unions and national services were decimated during the Thatcher years. In contrast, the privileged royal **PRINCE CHARLES** appears to have mined his

Venus–Neptune on the IC in Libra, spending much time building bridges (Libra) with the disenfranchised, unemployed, orphaned, disabled and elderly (all forgotten IC 'types' shown in his chart) through his humanitarian and charitable work (Neptune). With his Prince's Trust charity, he continues to help young people and the 'disadvantaged' (those who have been in care, in trouble with the law or unemployed long-term) to train themselves and develop their businesses (to become Aries MC-type entrepreneurs) and value (Venus) their talents and services. His work has centred around Venus–Neptune in Libra themes: the arts, architecture and

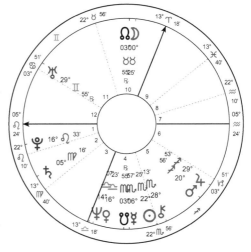

conservation/restoration, organic farming, alternative medicine, inner-city renewal and climate change. He has acquired a reputation as a leader in these areas (Aries MC) and even his Trust's royal logo resembles three rams' heads. (Venus–Neptune on the IC also speaks of the private torment, longing and sacrifice that characterized Charles's inner life and his relationships with both wives.)

MC–IC: Childhood Dreams and Parental Inheritances
Success ... is the distance between one's origins and one's final achievement – Michael Korda

'When you were a child, what did you want to be when you grew up?' That's the question my astrologer pal Sue Dibnah asks when she's looking at a client's Midheaven complex. Often the MC describes **early aspirations**, and these have strong links to parental influences. Sometimes there is a role in mind ('firefighter') or it can be more general ('I want to help sick people'). The MC reveals ambitions we latch on to when we see others doing an interesting job, as well as what was **consciously or unconsciously expressed by our parents** (it's very useful to consider the Sun and Moon here, too).

The IC is the inheritance point – the root and foundation of any journey we make out into the world. In *Snapshots*, I wrote that the MC–IC axis speaks of **messages that we received from parents** (or parental figures) that create **personal, deep-rooted principles** (IC) as well as **social ethics and work philosophies that shape our place in the world** (MC). As we grow, **what is inherited and instilled at the IC is called upon to be manifested through the social- and work-based lenses of the MC.**

Our first image of success (MC) comes from our parents: how they compared to other children's parents 'out there' in the world; how well our parents' aspirations blossomed. Whether or not their tree was 'in full bloom', the seeds of our parents' experiences were planted at our IC, and these nurture, cultivate, shackle or delay the development of the foliage and fruit that appear at our MC. (Not only can the MC show where our parents were in their own lives, the actual degree can speak of how far along they were in their own marriage by the time we were born.)

The Sun (father figure) and Moon (mother figure) in our horoscopes reveal the key images, impressions, facts and descriptions of our chief caretakers, but the MC–IC axis will describe the messages we received from our parents that relate to our own heritage and role in society. What were **our parents' ideas of success**? Were there heavy expectations of us, perhaps to carry on in their footsteps (Saturn aspecting the MC)? Was there an emphasis on exploration and travel (Jupiter–MC)? Was it important that we survive on our wits (Mercury–MC)? Was there pressure to be a golden child and fulfil our parents' own unexpressed talents and ambitions (Sun–MC)?

Whereas the Ascendant often describes the interpersonal skills we're taught as children in order to successfully interact with those around us (Gemini rising: 'Ask questions and find out'; Libra rising: 'Have good manners and you'll be liked'; Leo rising: 'Go out there and shine'), the MC reveals the traits that our parents thought were important in order for us **to integrate into society and survive and thrive on our own in the outside world**. Both angles express the messages we carry through life. I recall my Gemini father telling me to 'read, read, read everything you can get your hands on' (I have Gemini rising); I was also born partially deaf and my mother used to say, 'If you can't hear them, ask them to speak up' (Gemini). I remember leaving home for university and my father saying I should see my trip as 'an amazing adventure' (Jupiter–MC) – it was something he never had the chance or support to do. Beliefs

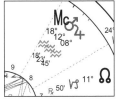

(Jupiter) were important to him (interestingly, he was an atheist) but the main principle he instilled in me was that I should have a social conscience and consider others – not to think of 'what's in it for me?' but to contribute, to make a difference, and to leave the world a better place than I found it. It's not surprising then that I was born with Mars and Jupiter in Aquarius and near my Aquarius MC. This describes many facets of my own life and upbringing but also reveals my father's lifelong mission as a well known personal injury solicitor who fought for the rights (Mars) of working class people (Aquarius) who'd had accidents (Mars) at work or on the road. Growing up, I was aware of his reputation as a fighter (he had Mars on the MC, too) whose nickname was 'Ruthless Red Frank' (he was also known for his strong Marxist and Socialist beliefs). As a union representative, he had originally fought employers for better working conditions and later, as a solicitor, took on insurance companies to get his injured clients huge financial compensation (in Equal houses, the Mars–Jupiter–MC conjunction falls in the 8th House of 'other people's money'). When Jupiter crossed my MC by Solar Arc Direction (SA) at nine years old, my dad made the papers and television news by winning the first ever million-pound personal injury settlement in the UK. This pinnacle of his career was seen in my chart by SA and made me aware of what is truly possible. (At the same time, I had just started my secondary education early and went to a school that taught eastern religions, Sanskrit and meditation – it began to open up my eyes to a very different world view: very apt for SA Jupiter directed to the MC in Aquarius, too.)

MC–IC: Crosses to Bear

I am not what has happened to me. I am what I choose to become – Carl Jung

If we identify too closely with the parental messages shown in the MC–IC axis, or if our parents expressed (or subconsciously expressed) needs that overrode our own, this axis can signify **the parental cross we bear**. It can reveal our attempts to fulfil **our parents' ambitions and desires** (particularly if a planet is conjunct one end of the axis) rather than our own. The MC–IC axis can show **our awareness of their expectations**: from the traits and philosophies they valued and what they considered important for success … to **what they asked of us** (and what the world asks of us now).

An ongoing debate in some astrological circles surrounds which parent 'belongs' to the 4th house/IC and which to the 10th/MC. Is the father the 4th because of his seed and how his surname is continued in the family line? Does it depend on who 'wore the trousers (pants)' in the relationship or who was the 'shaping' rather than 'hidden' parent? On her Skywriter blog, Donna Cunningham notes, 'The Midheaven represents the authority function of the parents and the [IC] represents the nurturing function.' I've written on this debate in *Horoscope Snapshots*, but would like to reiterate here that in natal astrology the influence of the parents can be seen *all over* our horoscope, impacting our attitudes to money, marriage, sex, work and so on. But the four angles reveal how our parents' social skills and relationship dynamics most influence us.

The MC and IC, the 10th and 4th Houses and the Zenith and Nadir

This is an appropriate place to discuss the differences between the Midheaven, the 10th House and the zenith. Firstly, the MC (and IC) is an angle found at one degree in our chart, while the 10th (and 4th) House is an area of experience spanning a number of degrees in the horoscope. In most house systems, the MC degree begins the 10th House and the IC degree begins the 4th House (in fact, each of the four angles is the 'cusp' of an angular house). In older systems of house division such as Equal and Whole Sign, the MC–IC axis can 'float' anywhere across the 8th–2nd Houses to the 11th–5th Houses. In extreme latitudes, the axis can appear in the 12th–6th Houses.

The zenith is a point at 90° above (square to) the horizon/Ascendant–Descendant axis, and is directly opposite the nadir (see the middle chart below). It is the cusp of the 10th House by Equal division, and can be in a different sign to the MC (just as the nadir can differ from the IC sign). The Equal 10th and 4th House cusps (the zenith and nadir) are exactly overhead (10th) or directly below (4th) the observer/birth place. Occasionally the MC and zenith (and the IC and nadir) share the same degree (at birth locations around the equator or when a late degree of Pisces/early Aries or Virgo/early Libra is on the Ascendant), but they are not the same astronomical point.

The Equal house system (EQHS) takes the exact degree and minute of the Ascendant and repeats them with each successive sign on the houses that follow (i.e. if the cusp of the Ascendant/1st House is 24°06' Gemini, the 2nd House begins at 24°06' Cancer, the 3rd at 24°06' Leo). Using Equal houses (where each house cusp is in exact aspect to the all-important 1st House starting position) would link every consequent house directly to the viewpoints, attitudes and 'reality' as seen through the personal lens of the 1st House ('my' appearance, 'my' approach, 'my' expectations). There is a subjective, personalized (Ascendant-orientated) quality to all the houses that follow (2nd House: 'my' money, possessions and values; 3rd House: 'my' local environment, 'my' siblings, 'my' school, and so on). It reveals our basic attitudes to all these areas of life and how we put our resources to work for us. Lois Rodden, after many years of using other house systems, concluded, 'The mundane patterns of the life stand out more graphically with EQHS.' I use EQHS but, for convenience, most charts in this booklet have been calculated with Placidus cusps (a quadrant house system).

When using Equal (or Whole Sign) houses, the MC and IC, rather than being fixed house-starting anchors for the 10th and 4th houses (respectively), will 'float' across a pair of houses. I wouldn't consider the house placements of the 'floating' MC and IC to be particularly important but they can add some weight to other factors in the horoscope. If the axis falls across the 8th and 2nd Houses, it could describe issues of

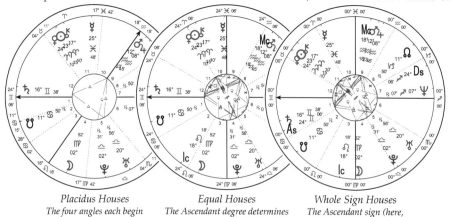

Placidus Houses	Equal Houses	Whole Sign Houses
The four angles each begin one of the angular houses (1, 4, 7, 10) and quadrants.	*The Ascendant degree determines all houses. Note the zenith (10th house cusp) and nadir (4th).*	*The Ascendant sign (here, Gemini) becomes the whole of the 1st House, and so on.*

family money and inheritances that shape the life direction; alternatively, it could suggest investment in research and exploration. Across the 9th and 3rd, there's a parental focus on education, ethics, foreign cultures or a need for us to create our own philosophy. Across the 11th and 5th the need is to find our community or create social or political frameworks. If the axis falls across the 10th and 4th, we may seek to build traditional family and work structures in our lives.

In her fascinating book, *Equal Houses* (AFA, 1991), Beth Koch writes that the MC 'rather than representing a house cusp, should be viewed as a distinct reference point in a chart, related to the direction in which you are pulled to fulfil your individual sense of self. It symbolizes more of a pivotal quality of your temperament, nature and sense of ego than the dimension of experience represented by the 10th Equal house.' She continues that the Midheaven 'represents your way of actualizing who you are and what you seek to achieve within the framework of society … It is symbolically your culminating degree of personality and potential. It has a great deal to say about how you feel successful, secure and personally affirmed in your activities.'

Regardless of whether the MC–IC axis begins the 10th and 4th Houses, it still remains extremely important in our chart and our life. But the MC and IC (the signs on the cusps and planets in aspect) are **psychological orientations we gravitate towards, attitude constructs and deeply felt drives pertaining to our place in our family and the world**. *They are not houses, which are realms, areas or environments of mundane experience.* The Midheaven describes our psychological motivations and purpose for having a social or professional role, while the 10th House itself (the sign on the cusp and any planets posited) can describe our employer and our mundane, working life (what we actually 'do' for a living). The IC reveals our psychological roots, family origins and internal motivations, while the 4th House itself (the sign on the cusp and any planets posited) describes our actual home, land and other 'fixed' property.

A transit, progression or direction to the Equal 10th House cusp degree (or a planet in the 10th House) brings up important work developments, while the same to the MC will coincide with something more meaningful about our life direction, reputation or quest for deeper fulfilment. A planet transiting, progressing or directing over the Equal 4th House cusp (or aspecting a planet while in the 4th) might indicate a change to the actual home or property, while a planet transiting the IC will have greater, more personal and internal significance concerning where we've come from, our psychological roots, lineage and family legacy. To an outside observer, it may manifest as a similar event, but the impact and its translation by the person affected is 'deeper' and more meaningful when the IC is involved.

Consider the Solar Arc Directions (SA) for **MADONNA** at two important times in her early adult life. In the first (1977–8), SA Mars moved over her MC. In the second (spring/summer 1982), Mars had reached the degree of the 10th House cusp and entered the 10th House. The first period coincided with Madonna leaving her home and family in Michigan and travelling to New York City to be a dancer (she also waited tables and worked as a nude model). It was a strike for independence (Mars–MC), to 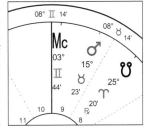 make a name for herself (MC) away from family (IC). She expressed the Mars theme when she said, 'It was the first time I'd ever taken a plane, the first time I'd ever gotten a taxi cab. I came here with $35 in my pocket. It was the bravest thing I'd ever done.' The second event coincided with her signing a record deal with Sire Records. It was the beginning of her ambitious, self-propelled, risky and sexually provocative entertainment career (note natal Mars in Taurus square Uranus in Leo) in its many facets (Mars crossing over her 10th House cusp in Gemini).

Lois Rodden taught me that when the MC progresses or Solar Arc directs to the Equal 10th House cusp (or vice versa), this will often be a time in which the life path is revealed or developments occur that change our job or place in the world; it could be a time of significance when a door opens (even momentarily). Lois called it 'a year of career or life decisions'. If the MC and Equal 10th House cusp degrees are close together, they will progress/direct at a very early age. We were too young to be working, but we were probably aware of a key change in the family structure or later heard that an important choice was made by a parent at that time. In Madonna's case, it coincided with a life-defining moment: her mother died when she was five.

The Sun and MC: Accomplishing Our Personal Purpose in the Professional World

The meaning of life is to find your gift. The purpose of life is to give it away
– Pablo Picasso (Mercury in Scorpio opposite Jupiter in Taurus in the 10th)

The Midheaven is often seen as a vocational point in the horoscope (perhaps because 'vocation', 'job' and 'career' are sometimes used interchangeably), but it's the Sun's message that is linked to the deeper meanings of the concept. In *Horoscope Snapshots*, I wrote a chapter entitled 'The Sun, Moon and Midheaven in Vocation'. I should like to share some of it with you here, and add that I am indebted to the work of Liz Greene and Brian Clark in this area of astrology. In the chapter, I wrote:

A vocation is something that gives our life meaning and significance; it occupies a place in us of creativity and fertility. It is something we feel compelled and 'called' to do (from *vocare*, to call and *vocationem*, spiritual calling). The vocation is a fundamental area of our life to which we are dedicated. It may have little to do with our basic job or how we earn a living. Our vocation lies within us; it is at the core of our reason for being/living. It is understandable then that some astrologers, including me, link vocation to the astrological Sun rather than a house or horoscope angle … Its link to the Sun in our horoscope suggests that our calling is something 'deep down inside ourselves' striving to appear, to make a significant personal statement and to stamp an individual mark (the Sun) in some way onto the world around us … The vocation isn't a clear job definition. It is what lies at the heart of the matter, the purpose behind the activity. Writing or composing is not a vocation per se. The vocation is the life force and energy *behind* the composition: the motivation that prompts a desire to write and communicate one's message. Astrology isn't a vocation either; it's a vehicle – a language, method, tool – to help us fulfil our calling. Each astrologer becomes a specific type of practitioner and for very different, individual reasons (as seen in their natal horoscope).

Unless our work is meaningful to us and an expression of who we are, none of us lies on our deathbed wishing we'd spent more time at the office! When our work becomes an extension of ourselves, our core beliefs and world view, we live with more authenticity and have the chance to experience life and work fully and vibrantly on a daily basis. (As the song goes, we live our days instead of counting our years.)

Then, our work rarely feels like 'work', pressure is a privilege and commitment is an honour.

In a section entitled 'Directing the Sun through the Lens of the Midheaven', I explained how the MC can act as **a master of ceremonies**, bringing together many aspects of the chart and channelling them 'out there' into society or a public, social or work arena. It plays an important role in the *fulfilment* of one's life purpose (Sun) as it helps us to express our personal journey and philosophies (the Sun) – our *essential* life direction – in the wider world.

Working the message of the Sun (the inner light) through the filter/lens of the MC (the external prism) is a way of fulfilling our destination/destiny/role in a social or public context. It is not necessarily about achieving acclaim or public renown – or even earning a living in the area of our vocation. It is about finding **a way to project our solar philosophies, purpose and creative desires through the lens of the MC in order to make a meaningful, personal contribution (the Sun) for the greater good of the world around us (the MC)**. It's about 'putting our vocation' out there and inspiring, helping, awakening, supporting and educating others. The MC complex is the signpost to how we can do this successfully and have others recognize our contribution.

Consider the Sun like a 'beam of light' (the *colour* of this light is described by the sign placement, the *source* by the element of its sign, and its *atmospheric interaction* from planetary aspects). Imagine it when projected through the prism of a particular MC – when it's refracted into society. The MC is **the most ideal way of actualizing the chart's potential** (as shown by the Sun in particular) in order to 'become ourselves' in society – it shows how we can bear fruit socially and professionally. How we manifest in society what we feel summoned to do is shown by how well we are able to integrate the MC complex (its sign and aspects) with the Sun complex. Are these points immediately compatible? Is their conversation fluent, the message easily accessed and understood? Do these two complexes require more effort and awareness to make manifest one's essential 'heart' (the Sun) and receive some sort of recognition and validation? For instance, it might be 'easy' for someone with the Sun in Aries to shine this through an MC in the fellow Fire sign of Leo, but how can someone with the Sun in Cancer shine through an MC in Aquarius? Still, any combination of signs, no matter how disparate, is capable of producing something remarkable and individual!

As mentioned earlier, part of the challenge of the MC–IC axis is to direct a spotlight on both angles, recognizing the 'programming' we've received from family and other early influences, seeing which parts belong to them and which are our own, and then making conscious decisions to put aside the areas that don't represent who we are or what we wish to be. We need to find the nugget of gold that is our vocation – the Sun – polish it and use our MC to find an outlet for it.

Life is pure flame, and we live by an invisible sun within us – Sir Thomas Browne

Steps to Delineating the Midheaven ♈

Using the horoscope of singer–actress **IRENE CARA** (on the right, with only MC-related aspects drawn in), let's look at the stages in interpreting the MC complex. Consider:

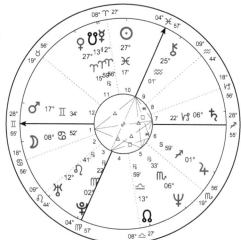

1. The **sign on the MC** cusp. *Pisces.* This will describe the general characteristics of the MC – and the many points discussed earlier. Take into account the opposite sign – on the IC – and the major themes of the polarity. Also consider the sign's element (motivation) and mode (style, approach).

2. The **ruler of the MC's sign and its placement.** *Jupiter in Sagittarius in the 6th.* This will reveal specific information about our MC. Look at its condition. Does it stand out? Is it heavily aspected? Is it in a sign that naturally 'speaks' to the MC's sign? The MC ruler is the prime energy – the tool – we have at our disposal to best approach and work with the Midheaven. The ruler's sign reveals the style, attitude and *colour* with which that energy will be expressed, and the ruler's house (the *where*) links the affairs of that house to the MC. If there's a modern, outer planet ruler (for MCs in Scorpio, Aquarius and Pisces only), consider how the generational 'seed' works in our chart; how we are inspired by the zeitgeist, how we are swept up, work with or even impact the larger issues and headlines of our era. *Neptune in Scorpio in the 5th.* When the ruler is natally retrograde, there can be a pause in our lives during which the goals of our MC are put on hold; we will be given a second chance later to explore these goals on more fertile ground and watch them blossom.

3. Any **planets conjunct the MC–IC axis** (within 8°–10°). *Chiron conjunct MC; Pluto conjunct IC (i.e. opposite the MC).* These dominate the axis and its message in our lives. They are more important than the signs on our MC–IC axis.

4. **Other planetary aspects to the MC.** *Moon trine MC; Jupiter square MC; Saturn sextile MC; Neptune trine MC.* Planets will usually aspect both ends of the axis, e.g. Saturn square MC and IC, but as we assign different orbs to aspects it won't always happen. For instance, in this case, the Moon is within its orb (8°00') of a trine to the MC but it is just out of orb (beyond 4°00') of sextiling the IC.

5. **Repetitive themes.** Is the ruler of the MC in aspect to the MC? *Jupiter squares the MC; Neptune trines the MC.* This strengthens, supports and quickens the message and journey of the MC (although the square can warn of challenges to the reputation). Or perhaps the MC has two rulers and they're in aspect to each other. Another way of underscoring the MC's theme is when the MC ruler is in its own sign or house, e.g. having a Virgo MC with ruler Mercury in the 6th House (a house linked to Virgo) or in the other Mercury sign of Gemini. Another example would be Libra on the MC with ruler Venus in the Venusian 2nd or 7th House or in the sign

of Libra or Taurus. In our chart example, *the MC is in Pisces and the ruler is Jupiter in the Jupiterian sign of Sagittarius.*

6. **Influential contacts**. This occurs when the MC ruler links to an important part of the horoscope, for instance when the MC ruler conjuncts the Ascendant (Chart) ruler. This is an aspect to pay close attention to in the horoscope because it involves planets that rule two important angles. In this example, we have greater control over our reputation (MC) and identify (Ascendant) strongly with it. We might be the face on the product we sell. Another example of 'being at home with our reputation' is when the MC is in the same sign as the Sun or Moon, the Chart Ruler or the Sun sign ruler (particularly when the planet makes a conjunction to the MC). In our chart example opposite, *the Sun and MC are both in Pisces.* Another point to consider: when the ruler of the MC is in aspect to a planet in the 10th House. Here, the reputation and public image are strongly linked to our choice of job (sometimes we 'are' our work) and the manifestation of success through professional endeavours can be easier.

7. **Decans**. The first 10° of a sign is a 'pure' manifestation of the sign; the middle 10° is co-ruled by the sign that follows in our MC's element's group (in zodiac order); the final 10° is co-ruled by the final sign of the same elemental group as our MC. Here's a quick guide:

MC sign	0°00' to 9°59'	10°00' to 19°59'	20°00' to 29°59'
Aries	Aries	Leo	Sagittarius
Taurus	Taurus	Virgo	Capricorn
Gemini	Gemini	Libra	Aquarius
Cancer	Cancer	Scorpio	Pisces
Leo	Leo	Sagittarius	Aries
Virgo	Virgo	Capricorn	Taurus
Libra	Libra	Aquarius	Gemini
Scorpio	Scorpio	Pisces	Cancer
Sagittarius	Sagittarius	Aries	Leo
Capricorn	Capricorn	Taurus	Virgo
Aquarius	Aquarius	Gemini	Libra
Pisces	Pisces	Cancer	Scorpio

What this means in practice is that an MC at 20'07° Pisces, for instance, will be tinged with a Scorpionic flavour. It will still be Pisces in most ways but the reputation, public image, etc, will have a more intense, driven 'feel' to it (Scorpio) than we would usually expect of Pisces. A Capricorn MC between 20°00' and 29°59' suggests a reputation for research, precision and detail because Virgo co-rules that decan with Capricorn.

These decans can be applied to any planet or point, and I would suggest looking at the decans of the inner planets (the Sun to Mars) and Ascendant and MC signs. If necessary, we can use our knowledge of the signs to fine-tune the birth time and adjust the degrees on our MC to a different decan. Sometimes there's a repetition that feels fitting: my own Ascendant is in the Aquarius decan of Gemini (20°00'–29°59' Gemini), while my MC is in the Gemini decan of Aquarius (10°00'–19°59' Aquarius). Ancient astrologers sorted the decans by planetary rulership, but I think categorizing by element is just as simple and more effective.

8. **Combining the signs on the Ascendant and Midheaven.** Representing both parts of our public persona, this combination shows how our agenda and expectations (the Ascendant) work together to form our image and reputation (MC). These are mission statements and personal mottos that we employ to get on and move up in the world. (It is also interesting to note how couples who work together have strong inter-aspects between their planets and each other's angles.) This combination of signs reveals our 'look' – how we dress up (literally) and present ourselves (from hair to make-up to clothes; colours, styles and textures). If we have an Aquarius Ascendant with Sagittarius on the MC, we might appear as an independent spirit focused on freedom and the future. We could look 'hippie' and alternative (Sagittarius) or rather superior and aloof (Aquarius), depending on which of the two signs dominates. But an Aquarius Ascendant with a Scorpio MC will appear darker, for this is where the sign of sociology and anthropology meets the sign of politics and psychology! When Sagittarius rises, the mix with Libra on the MC suggests a more glamorous, socially conscious appearance than the sensible, no-frills, studious image of a Virgo MC. I remember a class I taught with four Scorpio Ascendants: two students had Leo on the MC, two had Virgo. The two with Leo had big or blonde hair and came across as dignified, image-conscious and 'showier'. Their questions in class were usually about themselves. The Virgo MCs *looked* 'smaller', discreet, more analytical and went for darker colours in dress and hairstyle. They would take copious notes in class and their questions were penetrating, psychologically driven and insightful.

More on Aspects

Aspects reveal a dialogue between a planet and the MC. The specific aspect to the MC shows the type of dialogue: **conjunctions** (potent issues and themes that manifest most strongly in our MC complex), **squares** (concrete life challenges that spur us on to achieve or conversely block progress until we master them) and **oppositions** (i.e. planets on the IC: anchors or millstones in our journey towards the MC, and areas that require balance or integration). These three aspects are of primary importance, but close **trines** (under 3°) will show up in our lives, too. **Don't ignore trines to the MC!** They are lucky, 'right place, right time', easy, flowing 'gifts' – abilities that can be elevated easily. With a trine, the MC 'tunes in' and receives the message of that planet clearly and quickly – and we have an early awareness that the planet works well for us. Trines to the MC indicate early success or recognition when young, or opportunities that appear regularly to open doors for us. Trines help promote our talents and agenda to the outside world. They also act as our get-out-of-jail cards, or were the silver spoons placed in our mouths not long after birth.

I agree with astrologer Faye Cossar that aspects to the angles differ from aspects between planets. The former show our connection with the environment while the latter are dynamic energies between planetary bodies. Faye says that aspects between planets form an individual 'crystal' shape. The exact time and place we're born determines how this crystal gets locked into the cross of matter (the four angles) and results in a particular orientation to our surroundings. Astrologer Jackie Slevin, in *Finding Success in the Horoscope*, has a simple approach to reading the MC for success: identify, interpret and run with the planet that makes the closest Ptolemaic aspect (conjunction, sextile, square, trine, opposition) to the MC. She believes that it determines 'the path of least resistance to achievement'.

You may wish to include an angle as one 'leg' of an aspect pattern such as a T-square or Grand Trine, but aspects to the angles reveal more about how we can get messages 'out there' (like a public broadcasting station, as Lois Rodden once wrote) than they do a pattern in our psyche that forms an ongoing life script.

In reality, and when researching chart patterns or working with clients, I would suggest wide **orbs** for conjunctions – up to 10° – and 6°–8° for squares, but smaller orbs for everything else. Give the trine 3°–5° maximum, and only a 2° orb for every other aspect you wish to use. Keep in mind that the MC–IC axis moves one degree every four minutes and aspects to the MC–IC change quickly, so it's best not to rely heavily on aspects in charts calculated using uncertain or suspiciously rounded-off birth times.

The Signs and the Midheaven

Here's a concise guide to the main themes of each of the signs on the MC. Remember that the Midheaven reveals our:

- ♈ **Definitions of success and our mission**
- ☉ **Image and reputation**
- ☿ **Role models and traits we admire**
- ♒ **Journey from our parents and past (IC) to our path and profession (MC)**
- ☒ **Rocky road to failure: fears, shackles and neglected needs**
- ☑ **Highway to self-actualization: habits for success**

I've also offered some ideas on the various Midheaven and Ascendant (rising) sign combinations, which form our public persona (see pages 10 and 24). Taking most habitable locations on Earth into consideration (except extreme latitudes), there are 38 possible combinations (rare ones are marked with *). Always look to the ruler of the MC, for that planet will reveal precisely how best we can carry out the promise of our MC's sign.

🐏 Aries on the Midheaven

We succeed when we take up exciting, short-term challenges; when we become the sprinters who set the pace for the herd to follow; when we lead, pioneer, act upon life decisively and explore uncharted waters. With an Aries MC, we need a battle to win and we're often drawn to competitive, pressure-filled performance endeavours such as sports or politics where the goal is to be the first past the post. We need to be recognized as number one and crowned champion. With an Aries MC, we should strike out on our own because we're not a team player – others are procrastinators who slow us down! When we do our own thing, we chalk up 'firsts' in our profession (e.g. the first woman to be company president; the youngest to make supervisor) and are often the breadwinners in our personal relationships, too. We admire independence and those who have the courage to stand up for what they believe in, even if they end up standing alone. Richard Branson learned independence at age five when his mother dropped him off in a field and challenged him to find his own way home! He summarized his Aries MC philosophy in his book *Screw It, Let's Do It*. For some of us, the image we aspire towards is that of the boyish action man, a soldier of life and fortune – the hero who slays his own dragons and rescues the underdog. (If this is sounding very macho, Aries is a chauvinistic sign regardless of gender.) We may also be known for our sexual exploits and innuendo (the men among us will have a laddish fascination with women, sports and cars – crudely: boobs, balls and BMWs). I once had a client who was born on the same day as I was, but whose four angles differed. I wondered how he would appear with an Aries MC. He raced down my road in a convertible, pulled up, jumped *over* the car door, put his shades on and walked confidently to my door. I thought, 'That's how Aries on the MC does it!'

When others think of our life, they imagine us: travelling at a fast pace; having a sense of adventure; being assertive; racing against the clock. **We secretly fear:** not being liked; not having a harmonious home life; ending up alone. **Our early life:** many of us come from a background of unexpressed conflict with an emphasis on keeping the peace; where there was little impetus to change the status quo. This is to direct us to steer the helm of our own ship and to know that if we want something changed, we must be the ones to take action. **We fail when:** we give way to passivity, indecision, laziness or co-dependency; we're afraid to fight for our principles; we stay in someone else's shadow or play a supporting role in our own life. **We succeed when:** we dare to assert ourselves, stay self-sufficient and run our own life without apology; we move away from people-pleasing and appeasing to putting ourselves first; we pave the way for ourselves (and others) by being self-determining and settling for nothing but excellence.

Possible Ascendants: Gemini* (a focus on youth; a low boredom threshold; a pushy communicator); **Cancer** (an instinct for leadership; great tenacity; fighting for family and security); **Leo** (a flair for dramatic self-expression; magnetism and egotism; a desire to tell our story).

Taurus on the Midheaven

For us, success is building something tangible, worthwhile and guaranteed to stand the test of time. We employ hard graft, patience and perseverance to attain our goals. Slow but steady and persistent, we remind others of the fabled tortoise that triumphed over the hare. We create good fortune when we have a purpose and when we stick to our plans and maintain our value system. We succeed when we are strongly attached to principles that define who we are, and at times must take a stance against those wishing to impose their will on us or those who attempt to control us emotionally or financially. When we stand firm and refuse to be intimidated, and when we have a clear sense of what's right and wrong, we gain power and control over our journey. Along the way, we endeavour to be a 'rock' and act as an anchor for other people. We're in it for the long term and want loved ones and colleagues to know that we won't bail out when the going gets tough. We have remarkable staying power, resisting the early temptation to jump ship for tempting shores, and most of us manage to carry a workload that would cripple others. Although we must always stay aware of our financial realities, we should avoid becoming too fixated with the material world or allowing others to have control over our financial security. We can find joy and therapy in music, art, beauty and nature. Music in particular can be a saviour and often it becomes a career choice or pastime. We may also be known for our sensuality, our down-to-earth humour and renovation and craftsmanship skills.

When others think of our life, they imagine us: indulging in creature comforts (from the basics to the finer things); working with our bodies; cooking, massaging or sculpting; applying dogged determination even to everyday tasks. **We secretly fear:** the unpredictable; emotional chaos; losing financial control; our secrets being shared.

Our early life: still waters run deep and early survival issues may have left us feeling polluted, so we compensate by cultivating a professional life that is profitable, steady and secure – one that helps us to weather any personal storms brewing. **We fail when:** we betray our roots; we become riveted to – or bury – past emotional traumas; we resist the inevitable tides of change; we give in to laziness or over-indulgence; we focus only on 'getting our money's worth'. **We succeed when:** we become self-sufficient, industrious and purposeful; we reject the rat race and 'go natural'; we put our own survival first; we amass something of material value and permanence such as property.

Possible Ascendants: Cancer (issues around money, security, ownership and our body; building a safe nest; the loyal carer); **Leo** (establishing a name and image; career longevity; promoting our principles); **Virgo** (learning to value ourselves; establishing a steady routine; finding a balance between helping others and not being overwhelmed).

Gemini on the Midheaven

This placement is often found in the all-rounder – those of us with multiple interests, talents and careers. If we have a creative job, we're most likely to be billed with a hyphen: for instance, the singer–songwriter–actress or the writer–editor–publisher. Our professional name (or nickname) might differ from our birth name, and we enjoy dual personas or some other split between our private and public selves. The image we wish to promote is one of resourcefulness, humour and wit; others soon appreciate our ability to entertain on a number of subjects, even if our knowledge suffers from being rather superficial (the curse of versatility). We relish the witty anecdote, the sound bite, the pun or *bon mot*. When left to do our own thing, we are magpies, gathering together mottos, ethics and beliefs from a variety of sources and ideologies in order to build our own eclectic system of thought. (With Gemini on the MC, we know that when we borrow from one source, it's plagiarism, but if we borrow from many, it's called research!) A social butterfly fascinated with anything new, we're also the connector and go-between who can instantly give others a name and phone number for any request. We admire those who are intelligent, well read and articulate, as well as those who survive on their wits and land on their feet. A perpetual student of world events and important trends, we wish to remain innovative and contemporary – maintaining an image of youth (or at the very least a youthful *approach* to life) is of prime importance. We are attracted to jobs that offer mobility, short-term commitments, the freedom to travel and flexible working hours. Routine is important but we must have the choice to adapt our schedule when our mood or circumstances change (otherwise we easily become chairman of the *bored*). We enjoy juggling ideas, people, projects and views and have fun holding simultaneous but contradictory outlooks.

When others think of our life, they imagine us: talking about projects in the pipeline; finding ways to stay young; in dialogue with others. **We secretly fear:** others' judgement; falling out of fashion; appearing stupid, prejudiced or narrow-minded. **Our early life:** emerging from a religious, sanctimonious or moralizing background, we move away from superstition and organized belief to seek out the facts, become better informed and make up our own minds. **We fail when:** we close ourselves off to possibilities; we attach ourselves to a fixed belief system; we gossip, behave insincerely or lack a moral code; we flit from one thing to another without learning anything. **We succeed when:** we unite cosmopolitan approaches or philosophies and make these accessible and entertaining; we engage in study to develop our skills and expand our intellectual versatility; we doubt and then question the official story.

Possible Ascendants: Leo* (the importance of communicating with confidence; hands-on work; believing in our message); **Virgo** (the challenge of finding a specialism and abiding craft amid so many interests; controlling many endeavours and multi-tasking; adapting to precarious everyday situations).

Cancer on the Midheaven

Many of us with a Cancer MC will move into the role of playing caretaker or 'professional parent' in some capacity, whether this is in the social services, education or in some other helping profession. We succeed when we show genuine interest in the lives and needs of others; when we nurture and respond accordingly to those around us; and when we feel deeply about our mission. We have a hunger for closeness and bonding and seek positions of work that 'contain' us, where we can interact with our 'tribe' and develop a sense of family (this placement provides 'chicken soup for the soul'). The primal urge to play carer springs from the well of indifference, coldness, loneliness or isolation that was our early home life. Because of – or perhaps in spite of – this, some of us work or train with our family or get involved in caring for a family member long into our adulthood. Particularly for those of us who have Libra rising, we may 'do the right thing' for appearance's sake and secretly dislike the expectations of us to play rescuer or unpaid helper. We lose sight of our goals when we seethe with resentment as a long-suffering martyr. We are impressionable and care about the impressions we make. One talent is an ability to tap into what may be popular in the future: we have an innate understanding of cycles. We succeed by shrewdly anticipating impending trends, keeping a finger on the emotional pulse, and sensing changes in fashion. Some of us get involved in services or products that assist others in running their homes more economically or with greater comfort.

When others think of our life, they imagine us: taking our work home with us; creating and maintaining a family environment at work; playing counsellor to friends and colleagues. **We secretly fear:** isolation and judgement from family; not having attained a good social status; growing old and being left on the shelf. **Our early life:** from early emotional hardships, inhibitions or parental control, we learn to create a family out in the world whose members are interdependent, protective and supportive of each other. **We fail when:** we refuse to admit our underlying ambition for status; we attach ourselves sexually or emotionally to those who are indifferent to our welfare; we forget the importance of family ties and tradition; we elicit sympathy for our own gain. **We succeed when:** we adopt a role that enables us to connect to others on a personal, intuitive and empathetic level; we give love and encouragement freely without ill feeling; we set our own rules based on the principle of acting fairly; we play midwife and guide others through crises and emotional rites of passage.

Possible Ascendants: Libra (a gift for skilful mediating; advocating for others without getting emotionally involved); **Scorpio*** (being driven to transform our home and family life; emotional insight into our past).

Leo on the Midheaven

With Leo at the MC, we should aim to cultivate a dignified, even regal, bearing which commands respect and attention. Some of us automatically exude a debonair or showman-like image and even the shy among us have 'presence', flair and an aura of authority. We want to shine, but our more important work is to make a creative statement of singular distinction that reflects our individuality. Our path is one that melds self-confidence with self-awareness. To some, we appear to be superheroes who can quickly master new skills and handle career, family and relationships with equal ease. High achiever Martha Stewart (Scorpio rising, Leo MC) projected an image of haughty perfection in her quest to bring back the lost art of housekeeping, while Charlton Heston portrayed the epitome of virtue, leadership and nobility in a series of classic biblical and historical films. Life appears to revolve around us and at worst we may be known for our imperious self-regard even if we justify our self-obsession as 'enlightened self-interest'. Consider the regal, reserved Leo MC women like Jacqueline Kennedy, Linda Evans, Grace Kelly, Joanna Lumley and Joan Crawford who, in their own ways and eras, were luminous with an unmistakable glamour and majestic grandeur. Aretha Franklin's voice and its battle cry for 'Respect' resonated with the civil rights movement. In her autobiography, *From These Roots*, the Queen of Soul wrote, 'Some were saying that in my voice they heard the sound of confidence and self-assurance; they heard the proud history of a people who had been struggling for centuries.' With our natural talent for self-promotion, we are adept at creating an image of pride and strength, but this is a bravado that protects us from prying eyes or from revealing our insecurities. Once we've promoted ourselves, we may struggle to keep our private life from being delved into further. We fail when we promote an exaggerated or false reputation; when we cannot live up to our self-created image of integrity. We are at our best when we show generosity and support to our colleagues and when we graciously accept the part others have played in our success.

When others think of our life, they imagine us: living the high life and a Technicolor existence; being given the royal treatment. **We secretly fear:** being run-of-the-mill, ignored or inconsequential; losing or lacking status; being unable to make a personal, creative contribution. **Our early life:** from an ordinary or isolating early life, we seek to stand out and create something unique – to be someone special. **We fail when:** we use others without due credit; we move from being an everyman to believing that it's every man for himself; we take ourselves too seriously and image or performance becomes everything. **We succeed when:** we display courage and 'heart'; we embody personal truth; we realize our creative vision and inspire others to realize theirs, too.

Possible Ascendants: Libra (gaining confidence in relationships; charm and vanity; popular leadership); **Scorpio** (the powerful management and control of our image; discrete private and public sides; pride before a fall); **Sagittarius*** (promotion and salesmanship; evangelism).

♉♍ Virgo on the Midheaven

This MC is that of the detail-driven perfectionist who is efficient, skilled and productive. We know instinctively that 'genius is an infinite capacity for taking pains' (as Thomas Carlyle, who most likely had the Moon in Virgo, wrote). This is a controlling placement and we may keep lists of lists to ensure chaos doesn't arise and that our standards don't fall. Before any endeavour, we ask whether it will be 'worthwhile' and 'useful'. We admire order, schedules and systems; we see beauty in a job well done. Most of us have strong work- and service-based ethics. Success lies in us becoming a studious, humble and faithful apprentice; later, this dedication ensures we become a specialist – an expert in our field. Along the way, we learn techniques and crafts and how to be of service to the greater whole. Many of us have a powerful desire to leave the world a better place than we found it. **HELEN KELLER** spoke her own Virgo MC (and ruler Mercury at 0° Leo) when she wrote, 'I long to accomplish a great and noble task, but it is my chief duty to accomplish humble tasks as though they were great and noble. The world is moved along, not only by the mighty shoves of its heroes, but also by the aggregate of the tiny pushes of each honest worker.' With a Virgo MC, we would much rather be noted for our intelligence and perceptiveness than our hair and make-up. We also prefer to dress in an unpretentious way; our image is one of modesty, tidiness and presentability – we look like someone ready to work. At times we may be known for our idiosyncrasies, eccentricities, strange diets or ongoing health issues. Unlike some who retire from work *and* from life, with Virgo on

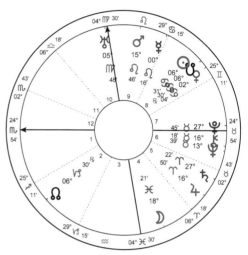

the MC it's essential for us to have a routine and to keep ourselves busily engaged well past retirement age, even if only on pet projects and the occasional bit of research. We should have days when we let go of work or trying to put the world's wrongs to rights, but we mustn't lose the structure that working provides.

When others think of our life, they imagine us: busy with projects that require an expert eye; honing our editing skills; putting our intelligence to the test. **We secretly fear:** getting lost in chaos; not being useful; being a burden to others. **Our early life:** from a lack of boundaries, addiction, martyrdom or chaos at home we vow to create a structured, systematic lifestyle and routine. **We fail when:** we obsess neurotically over the areas in life we can't control; we are aimless or without a schedule; we fall victim to fatalism and complain without ever taking action. **We succeed when:** we are of service; we use our skills to make our community a better place; we learn to give and receive constructive criticism.

Possible Ascendants: Scorpio (a detective looking for a motive; the obsession to control our environment and routine; perfecting our craft); **Sagittarius** (reaching out to serve a greater cause; learning and teaching a skill; analysing beliefs); **Capricorn*** (a long apprenticeship; supporting tradition; working within a hierarchy).

♎ Libra on the Midheaven

With this MC we aim to exhibit grace, style, good taste and manners. Displaying charm and getting along well with others are primary concerns for us. Usually friendly and well presented, we make excellent front-of-house people and meet-and-greeters. Over time, we learn mediation skills, decisiveness and how to meet conflict with assertiveness rather than aggression. We are popular because we know how to treat people fairly and with respect; but others may feel they've seen us only at a superficial level. Cooperating and showing impartiality are keys to our success; we lose respect when we coerce or manipulate others into lending support. We work well when in an equal partnership, each of us with our own skill set that enhances the union. At best, we can raise awareness of social issues of injustice, inequality and moral decline. We are often known more for our relationship histories and current love interest than for our own contributions; part of our life journey is to attain the self-worth and confidence to live life independently and enjoy the freedom of getting to know ourselves better while single. With her MC in Libra, legendary actress Elizabeth Taylor was more famous for her glamorous life, jewels and marriages than for her distinguished acting career. Her MC ruler Venus conjunct Uranus in Aries at the IC (both square Pluto) and her marriages ranged from passionate and competitive ('the Battling Burtons') to downright tumultuous. When she fell in love with a married man, Taylor was branded a home-wrecker who flouted 1950s social conventions but, in doing so, she helped reshape the social mores of her age. Whether we mean to or not, with Libra on the MC we end up addressing the imbalances of power in business and personal relationships.

When others think of our life, they imagine us: living a tasteful existence; socializing at cocktail parties; always in partnership. **We secretly fear:** our own capacity for violence, discord and dispute. **Our early life:** out of conflict emerges an ability to manage and negotiate strife with skill and subtlety; we learn to be the iron fist hidden in the velvet glove. **We fail when:** we create conflict and play people off against each another to keep our position safe; we act impulsively or refuse to compromise; we unduly prioritize our social standing or pursuit of pleasure. **We succeed when:** we form equal relationships based on mutual respect; we focus on similarities, beauty and fair exchange; we make love not war; we demonstrate grace under pressure.

Possible Ascendants: Scorpio* (negotiating relationship crises; the psychology of relationships; exploring and investigating the misuses of power); **Sagittarius** (speaking up for fairness; seeking justice; gaining confidence in relationships and break-ups); **Capricorn** (control issues in partnerships; examining class and status; working diplomatically in hierarchies); **Aquarius*** (unusual associations; taking moral stands; partnerships linked to humanitarian causes).

♏ Scorpio on the Midheaven

We attract much attention when we exhibit charisma and we succeed when we pursue goals with great intensity, willpower and focus. A talent for all-or-nothing research and penetrative investigation is suggested by this placement. We like to be seen as tough negotiators and skilled, political players, but we must keep the door open for compassion otherwise we can provoke much opposition. If we do attain power, we must manage it with fairness and avoid using it to scheme or to settle the score. Our lives are subject to extremes and fluctuating fortunes – vivid highs and abject lows – so it is wise to treat fairly the people we meet on our way up for we might encounter them again on our journey downwards. We have a formidable public persona, one that can be both intimidating and impenetrable. For many of us, our bite may well be even worse than our bark. We make astute detectives keen to investigate others' motives, read between the lines and shed light on what's unsaid, hidden or taboo. The biggest mystery to solve, however, may be our own. We rarely reveal to others the real person beneath our image and won't be exposed to the level of scrutiny to which we subject them. Wary of inviting intimacy, we maintain a 'poker face' and keep our cards close to our chest. Our vocational path may be linked to issues around life and death matters, illness, breakdown and survival. We are natural psychotherapists and may be called upon to speak about issues of gender, sex, power or discrimination. Sometimes, the death of a key figure in our early life proves to be a point of no return and prompts a personal or professional metamorphosis. Intermittently, we are prone to shedding our skin: abandoning a long-term personal or professional relationship and starting afresh – regenerating – in our pursuit of a more authentic role.

When others think of our life, they imagine us: courageously in pursuit of intense experiences; indulging in forbidden pleasures; testing ourselves to the max. **We secretly fear:** love without passion; stale routine; withering from boredom; losing our intense edge. **Our early life:** from a solid foundation concerned with mundane needs, we resurface as a powerful, enigmatic transformer who pursues the deeper mysteries of life. **We fail when:** we become crisis junkies always pursuing or anticipating the next drama; we stay in a comfort zone for financial reasons. **We succeed when:** we accept the compelling call to be the master of our own destiny; we assume a potent, transformative societal role; we dare to expose lies and corruption around us.

Possible Ascendants: Sagittarius* (investigating ethics; insightful ways of teaching; exploring philosophy and psychology); **Capricorn** (overcoming adversity; fighting for privacy, respect and control; transforming the status quo); **Aquarius** (the psychology of human behaviour; social battles around gender discrimination or prejudice; the power of a single voice to effect change); **Pisces*** (intense dreams and fantasies; a personal metamorphosis; empowering the victim).

Sagittarius on the Midheaven

Those of us with Sagittarius on the MC are seekers of wisdom and strive to secure a breadth of knowledge that spans the more mysterious and spiritual dimensions of life. We are natural teachers invoked to share our experiences of life generously and enthusiastically with others, but we're asked to remain humble by staying an avid, eternal student and serving a noble cause. Stepping into the role of guru, consultant or life coach is tempting, but unless we're conscious of our own dynamics this pursuit says more about our ego needs than about being of spiritual help to others. Rather than setting our sights on a final destination (attaining rank or status), we can live life more fully by revelling in the actual journey. With a Sagittarius MC, we know it matters not where the train goes, so long as we're on board. At times in our life we find ourselves compelled to speak up about an issue of injustice, corruption or hypocrisy. This triggers our inner evangelist and mirrors a far earlier time when we spoke our truth but were not believed. In taking up this crusade, we are able to fight for and show belief in others – to help them soar and to give them a voice. We excel at stirring up emotion in people and awakening them to their personal set of beliefs. We break down barriers and help others to see that we're all members of the same tribe, whatever our background. We have a flair for publicity which is paired with a voracious and contagious appetite for adventure. We inspire others to invest in their future by living fully in the moment and with integrity ourselves. We succeed when we set ourselves high standards of conduct and morality and stick to them. We fail when we preach one thing publicly, only to contradict this in private.

When others think of our life, they imagine us: travelling, learning and exploring; organizing big events; engaging in extravagant behaviour. **We secretly fear:** that life has no answers or meaning. **Our early life:** from a background of unanswered questions or mixed messages, we pursue the meaningful issues of life and the possibilities *beyond* the facts; we move from living in the present to considering how to shape the future. **We fail when:** we don't check the facts; we present superficial, sloppy work; we become the know-all, freeloader, name-dropper or con artist. **We succeed when:** we think big and prepare well; we promote an egalitarian, inclusive philosophy; we take up worthy causes; we help ignite the torch for others so that they may see the distant view.

Possible Ascendants: **Capricorn*** (the long road to freedom; the lone traveller; bringing new hope to old situations); **Aquarius** (speaking up for a group; highlighting issues of truth and independence; breaking down borders); **Pisces** (reaching out emotionally to others; dreams of travel and escape; learning moderation).

 Capricorn on the Midheaven

With a Capricorn MC, our path is to become a master or ambassador, to take control of our public image and gain others' respect for our accomplishments. In effect, we're really aiming to get to a level where we truly respect our own achievements and deliver what we promised ourselves early on in life. With this MC placement, we work to accumulate knowledge to advanced levels in order to become an authority; we create a reputation of expert distinction and respect. We may attain some measure of success early but our principal mission involves a long apprenticeship. The road we travel may be rocky, with some setbacks and delays, and may also involve the denial of our personal needs. We may also have to confront our attitudes to authority and 'the Establishment', along with our fears of failure or success – particularly our fears of not living up to the high standards we have set ourselves. We soon become aware of nepotism or favouritism: others have been given advantages or preferential treatment not extended to ourselves. Many of us are clear examples of the self-made person – we pay our dues – even if we do not consider ourselves to be ambitious in the standard, corporate ladder-climbing sense of the word. It's somewhat ironic that those of us with a Capricorn MC may start off as rebels (opposing parental expectations and authority figures) only to end up being one of the authority figures we once rebelled against (particularly if we have Aries rising: over time we move from outsider to elder statesman). The difference is that we achieve this position on our own terms: we become chairman of the board or get accepted into the private members' club having taken quite a different and more testing route from that of our colleagues.

When others think of our life, they imagine us: planning and building empires; working harder than our peers. **We secretly fear:** not having a loving family to go home to; never being respected for our contribution; losing control of our reputation. **Our early life:** we hold off from having our present needs met and instead embrace what's 'good' for us in the long term; we move from a traditional but emotionally entangled family life to developing self-sufficiency. **We fail when:** we wallow in self-pity or are consumed by envy; we sell our talents short; we place ambition before family or prioritize professional responsibilities over commitments to loved ones. **We succeed when:** we develop self-discipline, perseverance, initiative; we stay real; we go easy on ourselves and forgive our mistakes.

Possible Ascendants: Aries (working dynamically in society; establishing a reputation for excellence; changing the system from within); **Taurus** (being a symbol of endurance; seeking respect or control through money or status; learning to build and climb slowly); **Gemini*** (the young kid on the block who becomes the authority; learning to commit without feeling trapped; being an expert on many subjects).

 Aquarius on the Midheaven

Those of us with Aquarius on the MC feel different from our peer group – we know we just don't fit in. Perhaps we're ahead of our time or think that others don't question 'the way it is' as much as they should. We may have been cast as the 'black sheep'

or outsider because we are an independent thinker or not of the right age, class or background. Sometimes we're the only one in our family to go into a particular profession. Whatever we do for a living, we are never an average representative of our field – we are lone wolves and natural freelancers who avoid labels. It takes time, but we (and others) eventually accept that our unique take on the world is an asset. Some of us struggle against tradition and authority, blaming 'the system' for the lack of freedoms available to us as a community. But doors open when we accept certain social constraints and responsibilities and make individual choices that truly represent who we are (striking a balance between our two ruling planets, Saturn and Uranus). British working class lad Michael Caine (with Saturn on the MC in Aquarius) didn't have film star looks but eventually triumphed by breaking the mould and becoming a Hollywood success on his own terms (actor-turned-politician Glenda Jackson also has an Aquarius MC). Since *Alfie*, Caine has been typecast as the Cockney rogue or anti-hero. When honoured by BAFTA in 2000, he confided that he'd always felt like an outsider in his own country and profession. Aquarius is a fascinating sign because it's driven to fight for ordinary, working class people, but it doesn't want to sit down and be counted as one of the common folk. Its opposition to Leo makes it, at times, too superior and individualistic. (I'm reminded of the progression in *Animal Farm* from 'All animals are equal' to 'All animals are equal ... but some are more equal than others'.) With this MC, we admire and wish to emulate those who dare to be different, yet we must avoid being democratic in concept but autocratic in method. We have a fear of being ordinary or ending up buried in a field of seemingly indistinguishable graves, yet the key to tapping into success lies in understanding and communicating with the common man – never losing touch with that which makes us all human. Fascinated by the class system, pecking orders and hierarchies, many of us are keen to explore socialism, humanitarian causes or political activism of any stripe. We are genuinely interested in those things that set us apart as people. We're often seen as everyone's friend but we have a tendency to detach from personal involvement; in consequence we can appear cool, aloof and self-contained. In truth, we are known only to a few, close confidantes, and we succeed when we put prejudices to one side and treat the whole world as a family (where everyone is both special and equal).

When others think of our life, they imagine us: having a wide circle of friends; discussing the various dramas that arise in our family. **We secretly fear:** our life contribution amounting to nothing; being ignored or unpopular. **Our early life:** moving from a sense of specialness to *sharing* the spotlight and a purpose with our group; from self-centred passion and knowing what's best for everyone to promoting an idea that benefits (and is elected by) our community. **We fail when:** we act as dictator; we forget the human being behind the action or job. **We succeed when:** we take an individual stand for a group cause; we explore the truth without bias; we accept that we are more like our father than we care to admit.

Possible Ascendants: Aries* (fighting for the group; representing the common man; instigating social changes); **Taurus** (standing firm against bigotry; solid social principles; being a pillar in our community); **Gemini** (communicating a message with simplicity and originality; being an affable but detached people-watcher who enjoys biography); **Cancer*** (choosing an alternative family path; connecting to the average person; issues of closeness versus freedom).

Pisces on the Midheaven

This MC sign often renounces its youthful strivings for fame to find instead a path that offers some kind of spiritual practice. This is unlikely to be an organized type of religious doctrine, for we are keen to accumulate a set of eclectic life experiences and observations that can only result in a more fluid expression of faith, acceptance and forgiveness. Searching, searching, searching … Unless our chart harbours Mars-like drives, we may not appear to have a clear sense of direction but it's more important that we seek a higher purpose that offers us real value and meaning. Once we move away from early conditioning based on narrow mindsets or prejudice, we can see life as one awesome discovery after another. Sharing these revelations with others is our gift. Along the way we might attract Svengali-type people into our lives; there's a dimension to us that longs to be rescued and so we may inadvertently give our power over to others. I call this MC the 'rest cures, religion and pills' placement because many of us have spent our early years searching for nirvana in a bottle, Bible or bedroom rather than within. We have an impressionable, chameleon-like quality that mirrors the situations and personalities we encounter (we're able to be all things to all people), but being able to absorb, go with the flow and endure situations are our strengths. Despite our periods of disillusionment or despair, others eventually realize that we are survivors – we can live through experiences that would crush most people. But the recurring challenge of this MC sign is to avoid a reputation for unreliability, drama or escapism. Sometimes it's the crowd we move in that distracts us or the people in whom we invest our faith. There are occasions when we are labelled the patsy or scapegoat, which can trigger our fears of becoming the victim or martyr. If we complain of missed opportunities or receiving a bad rap, we must be careful not to use this as an excuse to live a life of resigned acceptance or negative thinking. We must accept that there will always be at least a vague mist of gossip or rumour around us, as our reputations and public behaviour arouse both speculation and interest. But part of our journey is to acknowledge the role we've played in constructing our reputations and to be accountable for the choices we made.

When others think of our life, they imagine us: being the Good Samaritan; losing ourselves in music; seeking time away from the crowds. **We secretly fear:** the inner voice of scorn, criticism and negativity; being controlled by anxiety, allergy or ritual. **Our early life:** we segue from strict schedules and work to becoming a poet and visionary who expresses ourselves soulfully. **We fail when:** we blur professional boundaries; we allow addictions into our working life; the voice of 'reason' overrides our intuition. **We succeed when:** we stop 'sweating the small stuff' and seek to connect to the divine; we show unconditional love to others and devotion to a meaningful cause.

Possible Ascendants: Taurus* (making the intangible concrete; a practical spiritual existence; financing dreams); **Gemini** (expressing our feelings and yearnings; multiple creative paths and talents; being an emotional and intellectual sponge); **Cancer** (tapping into the public need for fantasy; family drama; becoming the empathetic caretaker and rescuer); **Leo*** (connecting a spiritual side to our creative nature; having the confidence to dream; our emotional life as theatre).

The Planets and the Midheaven 🌳

The following examines the major themes of each planet when it is in conjunction with the Midheaven (within 8°–10°), but these interpretations are also applicable to other major aspects such as the opposition, square, trine and sextile. I've listed details above in 'More on Aspects', but here's a quick summary. **Oppositions** to the MC place a planet on the IC, where the focus should be on exploring our heritage; the challenge is to understand this theme and emerge as a separate entity from the family and the past (see pages 14–17). Oppositions, as mentioned earlier, can be anchors that support the MC's message or millstones that cement us to our IC. Mars on the IC could suggest an intense anger that either fuels our drive outwards or keeps us focused on familial conflict. **Squares** play dynamic roles in motivating us (if we understand and take up their challenges) or can play havoc with our reputation if a given planet's message is misconstrued. With squares, we are shown that in the middle of difficulty lies opportunity. Inspirational educator Helen Keller, who became deaf, dumb and blind as an infant, had MC ruler Mercury square Saturn. She wrote, 'Character cannot be developed in ease and quiet. Only through experience of trial and suffering can the soul be strengthened, ambition inspired and success achieved.' Squares to the MC often reveal what we attempt to achieve *in spite of* what was asked of us by parents and others. **Trines** are natural abilities that can propel us quickly into the public realm (e.g. Sun trine MC – we are noticed and offered promotion because of our inherent dignity or authority; Pluto trine MC – we are a master of reinvention, the 'comeback kid'). **Grand trines** involving the MC suggest success engendered by family privilege or parental support (or, in a negative manifestation, the squandering of family finances). There's at least an early recognition of what is required to step into our public role. Grand trines open the door, but the major life achievements – the victories won with blood, sweat and tears – are shown by the conjunctions, squares and oppositions. For more detailed explanations of these and the other aspects (including the quincunx and sesquiquadrate), see my textbook *Getting to the Heart of Your Chart*.

The material below is based upon research into the lives of clients, friends and people in the public eye. I've used some famous names in the text with biographical examples in the hope of adding to the understanding of the *essence* of that placement.

☉ The Sun on the MC

How many cares one loses when one decides not to be something but to be someone – Coco Chanel

The Sun conjunct MC is not a guarantee of success or eminence (nor is it overly frequent in the charts of famous people), but it is a sure-fire placement for us to receive attention, to stand out and get noticed. We have a way of commanding the spotlight, of being singled out and popular. Depending on the sign of the conjunction (as well as the Ascendant complex), such visibility may be welcomed or shunned by us.

Emotive singer **KAREN CARPENTER** adored performing with her talented pianist–brother Richard but preferred to do this behind her drum kit. Audiences wanted her singing to them front stage and centre, but with the Sun–MC in Pisces, she felt exposed, vulnerable and trapped inside a goldfish bowl. Karen didn't feel pretty or slim enough and her eating disorder (anorexia nervosa) went into overdrive. Tragically, Karen Carpenter, with her timeless, melancholic voice of yearning, became the first high-profile (Sun–MC) celebrity to fall victim (Pisces) to the high-achievers' disease.

One of the main points that stands out with the Sun elevated at the MC is an intense need for a personal life far away from any attention: we need to be left alone to be ourselves. It can feel as though there is nowhere to hide, and the brighter the (sun)light, the greater the need for withdrawal into darkness, solitude and privacy.

If we embrace the need for recognition, it is essential that image and applause never become our main objectives. Should we fail to live with integrity and authenticity, our behaviour might well come to stand between us and the honours that could have naturally flown our way. With the Sun on the MC, the truth will always out, so it's important to be genuine.

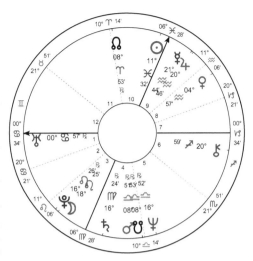

Many of us with this conjunction feel the strong weight of parental expectation. With Sun–MC, we may feel the need to carry and fulfil parental ambitions at the cost of our own. We might interpret their early messages that in order to be valuable to *them*, we must attain rank in the world or possess a group of qualities that makes us stand out. Our importance appears to rest upon our ability to shine or excel. If we show early evidence of talent, there may be additional pressure to be a prodigy; our parents may invest such great hope in us that we could start to feel that it's about *what* we are, not *who* we are. Part of a requisite of this placement's journey is to unearth our own vocation and to find the means with which to project *our* light into the world, as well as being loved indeed for who we are, not what we've accomplished.

There are some with Sun–MC who have become nothing less than symbols or figureheads of some artistic, social or philosophical movement. Most command respect and hold themselves with dignity and poise. Martin Luther King (Sun–MC in Capricorn) and Angela Davis (Aquarius Sun on a Capricorn MC) fought to change social injustice and introduce civil rights to American society. Filmmaker and satirist Michael Moore took aim at corrupt politicians and greedy business corporations (Sun–MC in Taurus opposite Saturn–IC in Scorpio). Anita Roddick (Libra Sun on a Scorpio MC) shaped ethical consumerism by founding The Body Shop. Baby Azaria Chamberlain's killing by a dingo in the Australian outback highlighted the dangers of gossip, rumour and media bias (Sun–MC in Gemini opposite Neptune, both square Saturn in the 12th) when her parents endured a trial-by-media travesty and were wrongly convicted in court of her murder. Actress Brigitte Bardot personified Venus (Sun–MC in Libra) but shone an uncompromising light onto issues of unfairness in society and animal welfare. Graceful tennis pioneer Arthur Ashe articulated his Mercury–MC–Sun in Cancer as he fought against racial prejudice. Recognizing the importance of moving forwards (MC) rather than being overly attached to the past (Cancer), he wrote, 'At some point, each individual is responsible for his or her fate. At some point, one cannot blame history.'

(It's interesting to note that we often meet people who have a great influence over our life path when the Sun is transiting through the sign of our MC.)

☽ The Moon on the MC

When lonely feelings chill the meadows of your mind, just think if winter comes can spring be far behind?
– 'You Must Believe in Spring' by A. Bergman, M. Bergman, J. Demy and M. Legrand

Like the inconstant Moon itself, those of us with this conjunction have spells when our reputation, fortunes and goals will markedly wax and wane. If we are performers, we may tap into a public mood or sentimental era in entertainment, but there will be periods when our popularity fluctuates: seasons in vogue and in public favour, then times in the dark and off the radar. The key to success with this placement is to understand the cyclical nature of our lives and not to expect a structured career or journey of steady building and accumulation. Life will be a collection of projects and encounters rather than a slow climb up the ladder rung by rung. (Astrologer Lois Rodden notes that each cycle is approximately two-and-a-half-years – the time it takes for the progressed Moon to move through a sign.) When it is the season to disappear, we need to withdraw gracefully and appreciate the solitude with which it gifts us. At our best, we can tap into the public mood or intuit what's soon to be fashionable.

We seek work that offers a two-way emotional dialogue (a 'nest' of a support group at work, perhaps) or makes a difference to the lunar-ruled areas of home, food, daily life, nurturance and comfort. Sometimes our job involves playing 'connector' or 'diarist' (particularly if Mercury or Venus is strong) as a personal assistant, stenographer, networker or media advisor. We are the 'glue' in any organization, a constant in an area of few constants or sure bets – for others at least. This is the placement of the *people's* hero or the public caretaker.

'Playing mum' – excelling at traditional mother roles such as cooking, caring, cleaning and 'containing' – is a powerful way of expressing this planet in the world, but much depends on the sign placement of the Moon and MC, for this will tell us *why* and to *what* it is we're connecting and protecting. Formidable British Member of Parliament **BARBARA CASTLE** (with Moon–MC in Scorpio) had a fluctuating political career of promotions and demotions before being elected to the European Parliament. With six planets (the Sun to Jupiter) in the signs of Virgo, Libra and Scorpio, she zeroed in with intense

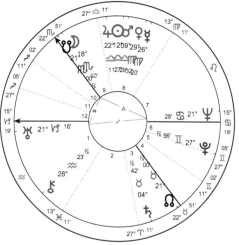

determination on the key issues of safety, equal pay, pensions, and welfare for the disabled and elderly, as well as the righting of several other social injustices. Preacher and broadcaster Billy Graham (Moon–Mars in Sagittarius conjunct an Establishment-directed Capricorn MC) stirred up emotional fervour with his rapturous crusades and via the medium of television was the first evangelist to be a household name.

This placement reveals an especially strong family impact on our lives and, in particular, a heavy influence from our mother in our choice of life path and social identity. A conservative horoscope may mean we follow in our family's footsteps, while a more rebellious nature will see us adopting unorthodox ways of expressing the lunar influence in our lives. Born into a high-profile family, Patti Davis (daughter of Nancy and Ronald Reagan) wrote a tell-all of her dysfunctional, privileged childhood and rebelled against her father by joining protest marches against his conservative policies (Moon–MC in Sagittarius, Aquarius rising). In *Me and My Shadows: A Family Memoir*, Lorna Luft (Moon–MC in Capricorn) writes of her nomadic childhood travelling with her famous, workaholic mum Judy Garland ('I never had any friends because we never stayed in one place long enough'); in recent years she has paid many tributes to her mother's musical legacy. Roman Polanski's MC–Moon–Pluto in Cancer – in a T-square with Mars and Uranus – is descriptive of some traumatic, violent and unexpected experiences linked to the mother, home and country. As a boy, Roman's mother perished in Auschwitz and he fled to Poland to start a new life. Many years later, the mother of his unborn child was murdered savagely by the Manson followers weeks before she was due to give birth. And, after being arrested for a sexual incident with a 13-year-old girl, Polanski fled America and remained a fugitive for 32 years.

☿ Mercury on the MC

As a general rule, the most successful man in life is the man who has the best information
– Benjamin Disraeli (Virgo MC)

Pour forth words and cast them into letters … For words have wings; they mount up to the heavenly heights and they endure for eternity – Rabbi Yanchiker

Mercury is the planet of exchange, trade and commerce. With Mercury on the MC, we are naturals in these areas, having been brought up to value interaction, dialogue and language and to question and analyse all the information we receive. If acumen is shown elsewhere in our chart, we may be renowned negotiators, agents or dealmakers; or we may be known as writers, reporters, teachers or instructors. It's likely that we will display a *variety* of skills (particularly if Gemini is in the mix). We need to cultivate a range of Mercurial skills regardless of our specific work. We should strive to educate ourselves and, where finances are concerned, to look after our own interests directly. We succeed when we view and approach situations from an objective, fact-driven and logical standpoint.

If the Moon is the emotional chronicler and connector of daily life, Mercury deals with facts, notices, data logging and processing. We are natural reporters and the sign of our Mercury–MC placement will describe what sort of news and information interests us enough to pass it on. (Mercury is easily coloured by sign placement and its aspects from other planets so the spectrum of possibility is wide.) In some signs, for instance Virgo or Scorpio, the information we amass, scrutinize and share may be research-based or elusive data that's critical to an investigative project. If Cancer or Virgo is strong in the chart, we might be collectors of memorabilia.

With Mercury on the MC, we're the observer, the voyeur who would prefer to maintain a healthy distance from our subject (unless Mercury is in a Water sign). It reminds me of writer Brendan Behan's attack on those who criticized his work: 'Critics are likes eunuchs in a harem; they know how it's done, they've seen it done every day, but they're unable to do it themselves.' And so the challenge for most Mercury–MC placements is to put our money where our mouth is: to *experience* life rather than to interview people or write and talk about it. Toni Morrison created a literary corpus for her community – lending a voice to the African American experience. Demonstrating her Mercury–MC in Aquarius, she wrote: 'Our silence has been long and deep … Today we are taking back the narrative, telling our story. The narrative line is the way we discover the world.'

With Mercury conjunct her MC in Libra (and maverick Uranus close by in late Virgo), Eleanor Roosevelt broke the mould of expectation by being a high-profile, revered and working First Lady. Even before her husband rose to prominence, she was on a social par (Libra) with him and considered a valuable, politically-savvy asset. Later, during the Second World War, she became her incapacitated husband's intermediary (Mercury). Eleanor was an activist, writer, educator and humanitarian who campaigned for women's rights and equality for African Americans. 'Send Eleanor Roosevelt' was the cry that came forth when Americans needed their best ambassador for an important occasion. With Mercury–MC in Libra, her most famous contribution was chairing the commission that drafted the United Nations' Universal Declaration of Human Rights in 1948.

With Mercury conjunct the Midheaven, we could well cultivate a reputation as a storyteller. On a superficial level, we're the ones who hear the information, the gossip, the facts – and we are sure to pass these on to others. The first time I ever spoke on the subject of the Midheaven, a colleague known for indulging in tittle-tattle about others' sex lives was speaking in another room on The Astrology of Sex – she has Mercury on the MC in Scorpio! With Mercury, what goes around, comes around, and others talk a great deal about us, too.

With Mercury in Pisces (on an Aries MC) opposite Neptune, novelist Jeffrey Archer gained a reputation as much for his personal 'mistruths' as his bestselling books, which he began writing following a financial loss in a fraudulent investment scheme (Mercury–Neptune). His most famous book, *Kane and Abel*, chronicles the lives of two Aries business rivals born on the same day (Archer's MC ruler is Mars in Gemini, the sign of the Twins). Later, Archer successfully sued for libel when a newspaper alleged that he'd paid off a prostitute. He later went to prison for perjury committed during that libel trial.

ROSEANNE BARR, a controversial, original and vulgar stand-up comedian, talk show host and sitcom queen, became TV's most powerful woman in the late 1980s and early 1990s as a working class 'domestic goddess' (as SA Neptune reached her MC and TR Pluto crossed her Sun). 'I'm your worst nightmare; white trash with money,' she warned. Along the way, she spoke candidly about her orthodox religious upbringing and her major cosmetic surgery, upset Americans with a crass performance of 'The Star-Spangled Banner' (as TR Uranus conjunct SA MC, and SA Saturn conjunct natal MC), mooned in public and devastated her family by claiming she was an

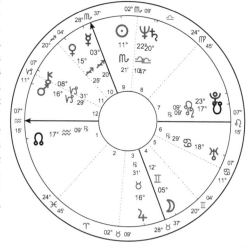

incest survivor. She later retracted most of the incest accusations. Roseanne was born with Mercury in outspoken Sagittarius on a Scorpio MC – and in Scorpio Sun and MC fashion, she fought for creative control of her show. She famously had a list on her dressing room door with names of the people she'd fire when her show reached number one in the ratings. A year after the show peaked, everyone on the list was gone – including the head of the studio.

♀ Venus on the MC

Be kind. Everyone you meet is fighting a hard battle – Ian Maclaren

With Venus conjunct the MC, we place much value on mutual respect, good manners, kindness, looking good and being an exemplary lover and partner. Vanity, charm and allure are three further attributes that might define us at various times in our lives. With Venus on the MC, we understand that diplomacy is the art of letting someone else have *our* way. This is *the* placement for those of us who are experts at persuasion, seduction or enticement – regardless of gender, what used to be called 'feminine wiles'.

We go out into the world looking to be liked and learning to please. And we succeed! We become popular and we're invited everywhere because we sparkle with personality (a strong Jupiter or Leo adds more charisma). But all of this acceptance and admiration can feed a need for approval, the notion that we must manipulate to get something back, or a propensity to base our worth on the opinions of others.

Early on, it seems essential that we get along with others, to put their needs before our own and have them validate our life choices. This is what we're taught to do if we want to succeed, so paradoxically we make it part of our life plan and self-obsession. But what about being liked for ourselves rather than for what we do for others? Another difficulty arises when we spend too much time comparing other people's lives with our own – this can lead to conflict, envy or hidden resentment. Eventually we learn to care less about the approval of others and recognize the importance of an equal exchange in partnership with people both similar and dissimilar to ourselves. In this journey, we become aware of different kinds of beauty, as well as appreciating that elusive, Venusian moment of bliss and contentment when we truly fall in love. With Venus–MC, one of our life missions is to get in touch with sensuality and intrapersonal (self) love before offering this gift to others.

Where Venus resides in our chart describes how we bring harmony to discordant situations; it's where we play peacemaker and find common ground. With Venus on the MC, the family may have needed a mediator – perhaps an arbitrator – and we accepted this role due to our ability to resolve conflict. (Look to the sign on the IC and any planets there to see from where the deeper motivation originates. If our Venus–MC is in Taurus, then Scorpio on the IC could indicate early events over which we felt particularly powerless. Our mission [MC] then becomes to help people build bridges that last [Taurus] and to prevent matters slipping beyond our control again [Scorpio].)

Unless there are heavyweight planets on the MC or in the 10th, those of us with Venus–MC may appear to lack gravitas and can struggle to be taken seriously (particularly if Venus is in the 10th). Some of us have periods of being seen as the partygoer, the self-indulgent lover (think of Jack Nicholson's image – he has Venus–MC in Aries – or nightclub owner Peter Stringfellow) or as someone's partner rather than for our own individuality. And those of us who take the hedonistic Venusian route might be known as 'the good time that was had by all'.

Party girl **CHRISTINE KEELER**, with Venus–MC in Aquarius opposite Pluto–IC, was branded a 'tart' for her part in the infamous 1963 Profumo Affair which toppled the British Government. She went to prison and the scandal sullied her name. 'Poor Little Rich Girl' Barbara Hutton, the Woolworth heiress, had the same angular opposition and her seven marriages and extravagance populated tabloid columns for decades. Sarah Ferguson, the Duchess of York, also endured intense criticism for her relationship choices and financial woes – she has Venus–Pluto straddling her MC in Virgo.

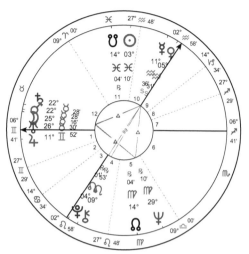

Often Venus–MC celebrities are packaged for a particular audience and sold in a one-dimensional way (think of the early careers of Brooke Shields, Uma Thurman, Loretta Young and Susan Sarandon, all with Venus on the MC). But they – and we – are much more than stereotypes. Marilyn Monroe loved reading Freud (he was her hero) and wanted to be seen as an intellectual (Sun–Mercury in Gemini) but her Venus–MC quintessential sex symbol image was what the public and movie moguls craved. Venus is the image of the sexually liberated woman but in 1950s America of witch-hunts and censorship Marilyn was hired to entice men to movie theatres and typecast as either a vulnerable 'dumb blonde' or a seemingly innocent gold-digger (Venus in Aries on a Taurus MC) who declared, with her breathy, childish voice, that 'diamonds are a girl's best friend' (Aries).

With Venus on the Midheaven, people's perception of our lifestyle might be that we are merely pleasure-seekers, but they may be surprised to learn that we are extremely gifted in building bridges, resolving conflict and uniting people. The nature of our Venusian gift will be exhibited by the sign in which Venus and the MC is placed. In Sagittarius, though the reputation might be that of a freeloader who parties 24/7, on a deeper level we might have a mission to spread the word, to get people fired up about a belief or to spread the love. In Taurus, the gift will be permanency, rock-like loyalty and the ability to relish deeply the beauty of people and of nature. In all signs, we realize that love doesn't make the world go round – love is what makes the ride worthwhile.

♂ Mars on the MC

The quality of a person's life is in direct proportion to their commitment to excellence – Vince Lombardi

Here, with Mars on the Midheaven, we have the embodiment of the ambitious personality in a rush to get ahead and chalk up 'firsts' or the young, know-it-all upstart who wants to begin his career at the top of the ladder. 'Oh Lord, give me patience – but hurry!' Luckily, though, when young we avoid being classified as obnoxious because we're unafraid of rolling up our sleeves and working hard. With this aspect, we have a strong sense from an early age of where we're heading. Former prodigies Tiger Woods and singer LeAnn Rimes have this striving, determined placement.

Mars–MC also indicates an individual who will fight for gender issues or has a strong sexual identity. Acclaimed novelist and biographer Edmund White, who effectively invented the genre of the gay novel, wrote explicitly of his sexual adventures and of his fight against homophobic oppression. He was born with Mars–Jupiter on an Aries MC (personified in the title of his novel, *A Boy's Own Story*). Stereotypical images of Mars–MC range from the bad boy to the randy youth or lecherous old man with sex high on his agenda (the sort of character played so well by Benny Hill, who had Mars on the MC in Sagittarius, along with Jupiter). We also encounter the adventurous crusaders and freedom-fighters (Mars–Jupiter) played on film by Angelina Jolie (as Lara Croft) and Tobey Maguire (as Spiderman), both of whom have Mars–Jupiter on an Aries MC. The quintessential Latin lover, Rudolph Valentino, also had Mars–Jupiter conjunct the Midheaven.

Maya Angelou wrote, 'You may encounter many defeats but must not be defeated.' We soon learn that life is essentially about being proactive, having the courage to dare and attempting the impossible. With Mars–MC, we fire people up, challenge prevailing views and can be provocative. We may be interested in sport, politics, the armed forces or climbing the corporate ladder, but without a strong Saturn we can suffer from rashness, impatience and a refusal to play the game; all these traits will prove obstructive to our fitting into a system or hierarchy.

We need to be self-determining in our journey and we work most effectively when in a position of leadership, calling the shots and negotiating uncharted waters. Our urgent need to succeed fuels our single-minded motivation. The important point to remember is that we do not get anywhere in life if we leave decisions to other people (and when we aim at nothing, we seldom miss our target). The buck stops with us. We know that it boils down to having the right attitude and motivation: Mars is essentially about excellence and on the MC we are perfectionists who want to achieve our very best. Our projects will always be stamped with our identity and we get results through the sheer force of our personality.

This is a pugnacious astrological placement and there's often a battle with those in command. At every new fight, the bell rings and there's a new opponent to go the distance with. Famously, Muhammad Ali stood his ground and fought the authorities when it was unpopular, risky and legally contentious to do so (Ali has Mars–MC in stubborn, principled Taurus). Activist Karen Silkwood took on a chemical corporation (Mars–Saturn conjunct a safety-/protection-conscious Cancer MC), an action that was said to have cost her her life, while Coretta Scott King stepped up and took over her minister–husband's fight for civil rights after his assassination (Mars–MC–Pluto). Sooner or later we are called to handle violence, learn to stand up for ourselves or fight for our independence. Both Mia Farrow and Loni Anderson have Mars on the MC and their very public breakups with their famous partners overshadowed their acting achievements (Farrow and Woody Allen had Mars placements conjunct, while Anderson's Mars–MC fell on husband Burt Reynolds's Ascendant). The public can brand ambitious women with Mars–MC as conniving or ruthless without considering their many achievements. Former First Lady **NANCY REAGAN** (chart on page 44) was ridiculed for relying on astrology and rewriting her past (Cancer) and was denigrated further by pundits for influencing the President. Yet the most striking aspect of her nature was her fierce protection of him (Pluto–Mars–Sun–Mercury conjunct the MC in Cancer). She was a devoted tigress – Reagan's staunchest supporter – who took steps to wisely eliminate those who weren't on his side.

Early on, the traits of decisiveness, independence, competitiveness and strength were stressed by our family. We're tough on ourselves because there's much to prove to the world, lots to win and a need to be seen as excelling on our chosen life path. Mars–MC success requires deep reserves of drive and determination; every step of our journey is hard-won. But Mars energy is either fully on or it's switched off (the warrior is either out fighting or s/he's resting and recovering back home), so those of us with Mars–MC must realize that the energy is both intense and sporadic; we must allow ourselves some leisure time away from the hunt every now and then.

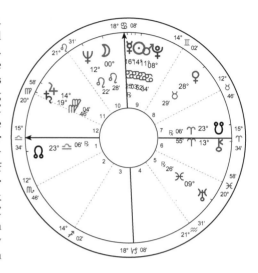

♃ Jupiter on the MC

Everything I touch turns to gold – 9 ct gold plate that eventually comes off on your fingers
– astrologer Roger Elliot (Jupiter in Capricorn on an Aquarius MC)

Although considered one of the most fortunate positions in a horoscope, Jupiter conjunct the Midheaven offers a mixed bag of possibilities. On the one hand, there appears to be much good will from other people – we benefit from their readiness to hold us in high esteem and to promote and invest in our talents. Our reputation can be made from affluent, influential contacts, and fortunate opportunities often fall into our laps because we're in the right place at the right time. On the other hand, we need to take care of our good name because any slip-ups, extravagances or reckless behaviour tend to be, in Jupiterian fashion, magnified, exaggerated and difficult to live down.

With Jupiter–MC, there can be an enviable confidence in our own abilities thanks to someone's early belief in us (this may be less so, for instance, with the conjunction in Virgo, where we may have been more aware of criticism and judgement than praise). Sometimes there are strong parental religious or moral convictions that influence us in childhood: an introduction to the bigger picture. Although this placement can be seen as an embodiment of the power of positive thought and the 'getting of wisdom', we may also struggle, like those with Sagittarius strong, with feelings of disappointment, disillusionment and depression because the world does not return our enthusiasm with the same level of exuberance with which we meet it.

With Jupiter on the MC, we want to have authority and wield power. Depending on the sign(s) involved, there can be an air of the aristocrat about us or even an overweening self-regard. Others may elevate us, convinced of our benevolent, altruistic motives, so playing God, guru, star-maker or Svengali is tempting with this placement. We succeed when instead we lead by example and help others to help themselves – rather than becoming a demagogue who exerts too much influence over our followers. The key to this placement is developing a reputation for integrity, high ethics, generosity and reliability – in short, a name for ourselves that is beyond reproach. Finding ways to be a Good Samaritan, philanthropist or educator fulfils much of this Jupiterian promise. Look to the sign of Jupiter and the MC – that's where our gift lies, the big talent we must share with the world. In Virgo, it would suggest being an important cog in the wheel as well as building a reputation for craftsmanship, analysis and editorial skill. With Jupiter–MC in Aquarius, we can be a generous humanitarian and educator in our community. As always with Jupiter, it's important to appreciate our fortune and to give back with open-hearted largesse at least as much as we received. If we persist in cutting corners, playing Scrooge, letting people down, agreeing to more than we can deliver or taking *advantage* of others' *belief* in us (Jupiter can be the *confidence* trickster), the magical aura of Jupiter and all it promises will be shattered. We can get away with murder for a while but when we *really* start pushing our luck, we lose it – and our reputation along with it.

With Jupiter on the MC, we may be honoured, elevated and lauded – sometimes disproportionately to what we truly offer (Jupiter is linked to promotion, aggrandizement and hyperbole). Some of us may come across as larger-than-life personalities. Consider Dame Barbara Cartland (Jupiter–MC in Capricorn), a symbol of old-fashioned etiquette (Capricorn) and sartorial outlandishness who was one of the most prolific and successful authors of all time.

Although honours and opportunity can come easily, at some stage those of us with Jupiter on the MC might have to fight for our reputation against attack. (When Neptune or Pluto is also dominant, it suggests full-blown scandal.) This can be a challenge over an ethical issue and may be blown out of proportion, but it's important for us to clear our reputation lest the matter overshadow all we've worked for. Jerry Lee Lewis (Jupiter–MC in Scorpio) was a celebrated pioneer of rock 'n' roll who found himself engulfed in scandal when his marriage to his thirteen-year-old cousin was revealed. His career never recovered. Disgraced MP Neil Hamilton fought accusations of bribery when TR Uranus and Neptune crossed over his Jupiter–MC in Capricorn; libel suits followed, which he lost, and his reputation was left in tatters. CEO John DeLorean (another Jupiter–MC in Capricorn) created an automobile empire that promised hope and benefit to many, but his schemes ended in bankruptcy and massive layoffs. Although he is still thought of as an iconic entrepreneur and dream-maker

(Jupiter), it is hard to forget DeLorean's series of business disasters, accusations of trafficking cocaine and the loss of millions of dollars of investors' money. And was Lee Harvey Oswald a patsy, set up to take the fall as the lone killer of J.F. Kennedy? Whatever the truth, he was murdered before standing trial. Oswald's Jupiter in Aries is on a Pisces MC (opposite Neptune exactly on the IC). Statistician **MICHEL GAUQUELIN** built up an *enormous* (Jupiter) collection of hard facts (Taurus) about astrology that scientists couldn't ignore. Over the years, parts of the scientific community challenged his findings, replicated

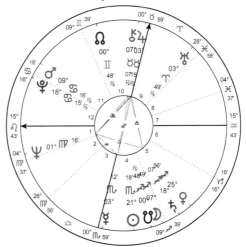

them (successfully, to their dismay) and then falsified evidence in a bid to disprove his original assertions (Chiron is conjunct the MC, too). But Gauquelin stood firm against decades of scepticism by fostering a stubborn belief in his findings (Taurus). Note Mercury in Scorpio opposes Jupiter–MC in Taurus, suggesting a penetrating, investigative mind, as well as the orders he left in his will to have all of his research destroyed following his death. His ex-wife described him as 'somewhat of a medieval tyrant – not easy to live with.'

It's interesting to note how many well known Sun sign astrologers have Jupiter on the MC or the planet strongly placed, starting with the best-selling astrology writer of all time, Linda Goodman (Jupiter–MC in Capricorn). The symbolism of Sun signs is very Jupiterian: these popular forecasts are published and broadcast to the masses on a regular basis, with the writer being seen (by some) as an influential media seer, modern-day guru or potent advice-giver who 'knows the future'. (Jupiter–MC contacts are also common in the charts of talk show hosts.)

♄ Saturn on the MC

Do not walk through time without leaving worthy evidence of your passage
– Pope John XXIII (Saturn in Taurus opposite the MC)

Astrologically, Saturn is linked to the acquisition of skill and the building of confidence over time; it's the planet of experience. And Saturn is a hard teacher, given that it issues the test first and the lesson afterwards. Saturn intones, 'You may not get what you paid for, but you pay for everything you get.' If part of Jupiter–MC's journey is to attain and then maintain integrity, the voyage of Saturn on the MC involves a heavy cargo of expectation and the requirement to steer always towards the island of responsibility and propriety. If we deviate from our course, we can be certain that we'll asked to account for our actions and to pay for our blunders. The consequences are heavier for those of us with Saturn–MC; downfalls come from not living up to a high code of moral conduct.

Both Jupiter–MC and Saturn–MC suggest an emphasis on learning or formal education. With Jupiter, it's about the joy of discovery while on a lifelong journey – it's rarely about the arrival. For Saturn, it's about reaching our destination at the top of the mountain with sufficient tangible results to show for our efforts. After some sacrifice and much hard work, eventual mastery of our subject is suggested by Saturn at the Midheaven; as Molière wrote, 'The trees that are slow to grow bear the best fruit.'

For some of us with Saturn–MC, the family casts an ominous shadow over our lives, as we can be expected to follow in parental or sibling footsteps, marry into the same community or continue to run the family firm. If our parents' ambitions amounted to nothing, we might grow up feeling the pressure to succeed to compensate for their failures. Or perhaps if success was hard-won in the family we have the compulsion to emulate this or suffer from guilt for not working as hard.

We may feel constrained by the demands of others as well as our own narrow frame of reference. Keeping up with the Joneses may ensure some measure of material accumulation but at what cost to our own desires? We only truly succeed when we divest ourselves of other people's images of success and instead seek authentic self-expression in our community and profession. Our goals should be to create our own moral compass, avoid living our life according to others' codes and to consider alternatives to what already feels set in stone. It may be a long apprenticeship, but it must be ours to determine and follow through. We fail when we stop daring to improve ourselves and when our fears and control issues override all else.

In Britain, we prefer our leaders and monarchs to reflect the solid and familiar edifice of Saturn, even if a Jupiterian head of state might offer more charisma, expansiveness and geniality. With a public image that's impenetrable, stoic and service-orientated, Queen Elizabeth II personifies Saturn on the MC in Scorpio. For her, being a monarch is an unyielding job for life, a commitment to be of service which requires a stringent, unbending moral code. But her reign has occurred in rapidly morphing times that have seen the slow death of tradition (Saturn in Scorpio at the apex of a T-square with Mars–Jupiter opposite Neptune) and a reduction in the prestige and influence of the British monarchy. (For more on her life-defining T-square, see my *Heart* book.)

Saturn–MC (or, indeed, Saturn angular in general) is linked to catchphrases and typecasting (a way to pigeonhole and *confine* others into a recognizable *category* because of their *appropriateness*). With Saturn elevated, it's not easy to escape the labels others place upon us, particularly if we have a talent that's versatile or we outgrow an image that was once assigned to us. Think of *Cockney actor* Michael 'not a lot of people know that' Caine, *intense spoon-bender* Uri Geller, *camp 'Are You Being Served?' icon* John 'I'm free' Inman, *statuesque Catwoman* Julie Newmar, *zany, neurotic character actor* Gene Wilder, *little-girl-voiced Sondheim songbird* Bernadette Peters, *wholesome teen box office star turned forgotten adult* Mickey Rooney, and the *daughter of Bing and the 'one who shot J.R.'*, Mary Crosby.

Oscar Wilde's Saturn–MC in Gemini is reflected in two of his most celebrated works. In *The Importance of Being Earnest*, Wilde satirizes the trivialities of Victorian society – its social obligations and matrimonial rites – in a farce of misunderstandings and memorable rhetoric. In *The Picture of Dorian Gray*, a narcissistic hedonist makes an unholy pact to remain young (Gemini) and leads a double life as refined aesthete and coarse criminal. In my volume, *Humour in the Horoscope* (Flare, 2014), I wrote that Wilde's 'famous epigrams and delicious *bons mots* sought to question social morality, and he dazzled the London scene with his erudition and ability to shock and titillate.' I added that Wilde had 'an unshakeable belief in his own intelligence, which would lead to his premature downfall ... Ruthlessly cut down in his prime, Wilde's Saturn in Gemini

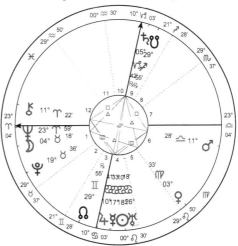

on the MC suggests his commentary on society and its manners but also that he was held up as an example and crucified by the high society he so wittily entertained.'

A strong Saturn can suggest a need for respect, privacy and intense spells of solitude. With Saturn, we also play time-keeper for people or may have an obsession with the passing of time. **MARCEL PROUST**, author of a seven-volume Saturn-titled novel, *In Search of Lost Time* (originally entitled *Remembrance of Things Past*), had the conjunction in Capricorn opposite Jupiter on the IC. Expressing this angular Jupiter–Saturn, he wrote, 'We don't receive wisdom; we must discover it for ourselves after a journey that no one can take for us or spare us' and 'The only real voyage of discovery consists not in seeking new landscapes but in having new eyes.'

⛢ Uranus on the MC

How wonderful it is that nobody need wait a single moment before starting to improve the world
– Anne Frank (Uranus–MC in Aries)

This conjunction marks us out as different in our approach, style or appearance – and usually not in subtle ways. We may seem poles apart from our peers or relatives or even feel born into the wrong family, country or point in history. For any number of reasons, we're not of our current place or time and may march to a different drummer.

This is the aspect of natural freelancers, those who are blessed with being freedom-focused and future-orientated. At best, we're actively encouraged by our parents to follow the road less travelled and to stamp our individual mark on society (perhaps because they were not able to do this themselves). But sometimes our experience of our differentness is less reassuring: we're singled out or even abused for our idiosyncrasies. We might choose either to withdraw or to build a social identity that's defiantly contrary and provocative. Whichever way it goes, with this aspect we somehow manage to rebel against our parental conditioning and expectations.

Our lives are marked by catalysts – sudden jolting experiences that take us from one path to a very different role or field; later we become catalysts for change in other people's lives, showing the benefits of personal freedom and demonstrating the importance of doing things our own way. Eccentric Phyllis Diller (Uranus–MC in Aquarius) was a married housewife of 37 when she buried the ironing in the backyard and took her comedy show on the road (at the time, TR Uranus was conjunct her Sun in Cancer). She opened doors for a generation of female comedians. A chance to sing at a club in front of Ike Turner took country girl Anna Mae (born Martha Nell) Bullock – twice abandoned by her parents – into the world of rhythm and blues to eventually become the lioness of rock 'n' roll: Tina Turner (Uranus–MC in Taurus, Leo rising, see page 11). Often, out of the blue circumstances 'blow up' and change the course of our life altogether. With Uranus–MC in Gemini, it was the sudden deaths of two (Gemini) loved ones that made Rajiv Gandhi the Prime Minister of India. Brother Sanjay had carried the family's political hopes until a plane crash claimed his life. Rajiv was encouraged to enter politics soon after and, upon his mother's assassination, took over her role as PM. After five turbulent years, he lost power but was on the campaign trail again two years later when he, too, was assassinated.

Along our journey, there may be disruptions, reversals, break-ups, breakdowns or breakthroughs. There is usually some subjugation or pressure to conform that acts as the trigger of our rebellion and break for freedom. With Uranus–MC, others are rarely indifferent to us; we polarize people with our public behaviour and the stances we take. Pointing out that the emperor's got no clothes often incites censorship, blacklisting or isolation; we have after all violated the comfort zones of those in 'the System'.

Once we've hit our stride, most of us are not prepared to veer off course. Uranus compels us to hold firm to our truth and adopt a radical, unemotional stance; being less than genuine is anathema to us. Anita Bryant (Venus–Uranus on the MC in Taurus) went from competing in beauty pageants and recording albums to declaring war on the homosexual community of the USA ... and on to filing for bankruptcy from the fallout in her popularity. Actress-turned-activist Vanessa Redgrave (Uranus–MC in Taurus) portrayed a series of persecuted outsiders on stage and film but is more famous for remaining defiant in the face of hostility after making outspoken, incendiary remarks against right-wing groups. Bernard Manning (Uranus–MC in Aries) created a crudely chauvinistic and racist public persona as a stand-up comedian before finally being banned from TV and bookstores in times of burgeoning political correctness. He once commented, 'In private, people tell the sort of jokes I do.'

It's always interesting to note that Uranus is prominent in the horoscopes of activists on both the far left and far right of the political spectrum – each side espouses vivid ideologies concerning civil liberties and freedom of speech. With Uranus on the MC, we give the impression of being either intolerant or intolerant of intolerance, which still makes us intolerant! In 1979, the newly elected President of Brazil made this most Uranian of statements, 'I intend to open this country up to democracy and anyone who is against that, I will jail, I will crush!'

Ideally, when we become aware that we don't fit in, we should remould ourselves to express what it is that we *do* stand for, rather than what we oppose. Then something authentic can emerge from us. At best, we can offer the world an aspect of ourselves that is exhilaratingly original and that helps others wake up to their own true selves.

Uranus–MC is very on-off, so our contribution is rarely consistent. It's important not to cultivate a reputation of erratic or eccentric behaviour (two unpredictable women who gave a series of electrifying performances in their careers, Judy Garland and Vivien Leigh, had this conjunction). Author **QUENTIN CRISP** spoke his Uranus–MC in Capricorn when he wrote the first line of his autobiography, *The Naked Civil Servant*: 'From the dawn of my history I was so disfigured by the characteristics of a certain kind of homosexual person that, when I grew up, I realized that I could not ignore my predicament.' Always the quintessential outsider, Crisp suffered years of abuse from the public before being celebrated as a one-off, a 'Stately Homo of England'. Understanding that most 'deviant' aspects of human nature become more palatable over time (what was once original – Uranus

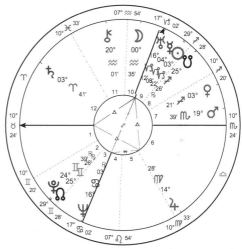

– becomes commonplace – Saturn), Crisp once remarked, 'Time is on the side of the outcast. Those who once inhabited the suburbs of human contempt find that without changing their address they eventually live in the metropolis.'

Two memorable 20th-century talents, educator Helen Keller and diarist Anne Frank, had this conjunction and both made remarkable, highly individual contributions to the human race while subject to extreme pressure, prejudice and incapacity. With the conjunction in Virgo, Keller wrote, 'The highest result of education is tolerance.' With Uranus–MC in self-determining Aries, Anne wrote, 'Parents can only give good advice or put them on the right paths, but the final forming of a person's character lies in their own hands.'

♆ Neptune on the MC

It is only with the heart that one can see rightly; what is essential is invisible to the eye
– The Little Prince by Antoine de Saint-Exupéry

Neptune's position in our charts tells us how we yearn to escape the mundane and connect to the divine. At best, those of us with Neptune–MC can offer others an insight into the spiritual realm or even help them transcend to a higher realm of creativity. This could be through our own expressions of art, music, photography, film, image, design or any other Neptunian pursuit. Although there are many possible creative outlets for our abilities, Neptune softens or blurs the drive to succeed and it often takes other factors in the chart to make these talents financially viable or marketable.

With this placement we can be beleaguered by aimlessness, uncertainty or vocational ambivalence. Neptune is about illusions and delusions. How can we become something in life if we don't know who we are? What have we got to offer? Which direction should we take? As impressionable beings and chameleons, we are influenced and swayed by the myriad messages we encounter. We may have big dreams of a future characterized by glamour, romance and celebrity but, without a lottery win or an overnight discovery, how can we turn those aspirations into reality? Or if we choose the road of spirituality, how can we charge appropriately for our time and services in order to survive and thrive in the everyday world? For those of us with Neptune–MC, there are many yearnings and lots of questions but seemingly few realistic answers.

One way of reconciling everyday survival with lofty spiritual goals can be through service to a cause: giving some of our time and energy to charities and voluntary organizations. The thirst to do something meaningful can be quenched when we engage in deeds that help attend to and rescue those in great need. By doing so, we can inspire people to move mountains with their faith and to see beyond the mundane. Delving into the metaphysical realm is another way to experience and share some of the greater mysteries of the world around us.

Sometimes Neptune–MC (like aspects between the Sun and Neptune) is present in the charts of those of us who had an emotionally or physically absent parent. This could have left the other parent feeling victimized or martyred. We connect to the loss and sadness of both experiences. For some of us, there was an addiction in the family that overshadowed our early life, or there was a mystery about our parentage or roots. In other instances, we idealize a parent or hanker after the 'perfect family' that so many other people appear to have. With Neptune on the MC, we can delude ourselves into believing there is an ideal that's only 'out there', away from us, beyond our reach. As a result of this familial void, we may find ourselves projecting an aura of sadness or suffering – or, in extreme contrast, becoming adept at glossing over our real emotions. For most of us, a need for regular seclusion and withdrawal is paramount.

This is an enigmatic placement and it's not unusual for some of us to be the subject of gossip or unfounded speculation. Neptune is linked to scandal and the leaking of confidential information (tabloid tycoon Rupert Murdoch is a Pisces with Neptune–MC in Virgo). With this placement, we might come across as mysterious, surreal, fascinating or weird, prompting others to revel in discussing our behaviour. We can dominate conversations without even being present. Iconic model Naomi Campbell (Neptune–MC) is often in the news for her alleged (a perfect Neptune word) demanding behaviour. Billy Tipton was a musician who married four times. It was not until his post-mortem that it was discovered that Billy was really a woman – someone who had assumed the opposite gender so as to be accepted in the jazz world of the 1930s and 1940s. This revelation left his wives and adopted sons bewildered – they hadn't had the slightest suspicion that their husband and father was female. Peter Sutcliffe terrified the British public as the elusive Yorkshire Ripper before eventually being caught. We all knew of the sobriquet but for years didn't know his identity (Neptune–MC).

Notorious madam **HEIDI FLEISS** (Neptune–MC in Scorpio) had Hollywood buzzing when she was arrested on pandering and money laundering charges in 1993. She had run the celebrity town's most successful prostitution ring for a number of years; her power extended to playing matchmaker for the richest men in the world, pairing them with women tailored for their every fantasy. But the Neptune–MC question was: would she or wouldn't she reveal the names of those in her Little Black Book? With her conjunction in Scorpio, so far she hasn't. Three Neptune cycles earlier, statesman Niccolo Machiavelli

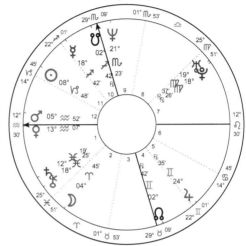

(Neptune–MC in Scorpio) presciently taught us that 'the end justifies the means'. To this day, his name is mythical in its links to intrigue, treachery and ruthlessness.

Irvine Welsh, writer of *Trainspotting*, *Ecstasy*, *Filth* and *Glue*, offers social commentary on the dark recesses of disaffected 'low-lifes' in Scotland. With Neptune conjunct Welsh's MC in the sign of Scorpio, he presents us with nihilism, deprivation, drug use and addiction with stark and unflinching realism. A recurring theme is attempting to escape the banalities of life by being immersed in a drug culture.

A positive expression of Neptune on the Midheaven is personifying an ideal to our community or even riding on a wave of nostalgia. Through cartoons, films and theme parks, Walt Disney (Neptune in Cancer on a Gemini MC) created a world of fantastical escape for millions, but there has been much speculation about the man behind the image. Neptune–MC aspects certainly give us a longevity we might not have otherwise enjoyed. Consider the mythical, sometimes shady, reputations of legends (another Neptunian word) Frank Sinatra, 'playboy prince' Aly Khan, Ayrton Senna, Clint Eastwood, Bruce Lee and diarist Anais Nin, all Neptune–MC. John and Jackie Kennedy's time at the White House was idealized and later encapsulated into one word: Camelot. Both had Neptune on the MC and their private lives kept the tabloids busy for years. At our best, we can take inspiration from other Neptune–MC people to keep our goals alive, for we must never lose sight of dreaming the impossible dream.

♀ Pluto on the MC

The only way to predict the future is to have power to shape the future – Eric Hoffer

The key to making the best of Pluto on the Midheaven is to harness the power we have as individuals as well as the resources that lie in the world around us. When I think of Pluto, I think of The Serenity Prayer ('Grant me the serenity to accept the things I cannot change, the courage to change the things I can, and the wisdom to know the difference'). This is particularly apt for those of us who live with Pluto on the MC. Unlocking the personal power that Pluto represents for each of us is dependent on our ability to know what we can and cannot control – both inside and around us.

Pluto is both the empowered and the subjugated; the controllers and the disenfranchised. For many with a Pluto–MC conjunction, there will be a haunting experience of loss of control in early life, a helplessness that makes us aware of the importance of controlling our destiny. We can either choose to feel victimized by this event or put vulnerability to one side and begin to amass power as we move through adulthood.

There may be several experiences of wipeout where we perceive everything as gone – our old life is no longer there and we must start afresh. Pluto–MC grants us the strength to reinvent ourselves, to rise from the ashes and transform our reputation. Coretta Scott King had Pluto and Mars flanking the MC natally and found her life swept up by the civil rights movement before and after her husband's assassination. Louise Woodward (Pluto–MC in Libra) was a nineteen-year-old British nanny on trial in the US for the murder of a baby in her care. After her conviction, she sought to hide from the intrusive glare of publicity and trained for a while as a lawyer, but the trial overshadowed her life and reputation. Unflappable prosecutor Marcia Clark (Mars–Pluto–MC in Leo) took on fallen sports hero O.J. Simpson in the 'trial of the century' and her life was never the same again.

CAROLE KING wrote and recorded *Tapestry*, a collection of songs that spoke to the everywoman (Sun–Mercury in Aquarius) and became one of the most successful albums of all time. This pop phenomenon (Venus opposite Pluto–MC) heralded the rebirth of the singer–songwriter as poet.

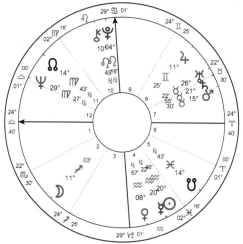

For some with Pluto–MC, there is in the closet a family event or skeleton whose emergence shakes us to our foundations. It is often the case that our motivation to be in control originated from a powerful parent dominating us – or feeling their overwhelming desire for us to live out their unfulfilled ambitions. Here we have the image of the parent pushing their kid onto court or a stage at age five. Tennis star Chris Evert has this conjunction and she says that, for the longest time, her identity and self-esteem were defined by winning or losing a match.

Pluto–MC is linked to fields such as psychology and psychiatry – in-depth explorations of the usually hidden sides of the psyche. I have come across many clients working in dangerous or taboo areas who have this placement. One was a female psychotherapist (with Scorpio rising) working in a maximum security prison for some of the most violent male criminals in America. It takes an unflinching character with great psychological perspicacity to work in such an environment. (The Pluto–MC and Scorpio rising combination is also common in those who combine sex with their image: consider the charts of prostitute-turned-MP Ilona Staller/Cicciolina; romance novel cover-boy Fabio; and innovative singer-songwriter Prince, known for his explicit videos and lyrics. Prince fought a long Pluto battle with his record label, during which he changed his name to a symbol and wrote 'slave' on his cheek.)

A need to exert influence over our environment is combined with a desire for privacy and seclusion. This is a placement linked to people who exert power behind the throne; we're more likely to find plutocrats and the owners of the means of production with this aspect than celebrities or other people on the frontline. And with Pluto, our public image is often very different to who we are in our personal lives.

At best, we can work to help those who have suffered trauma or violation; to give a hand to the victimized, persecuted or abused. This is a placement that suggests a need to regularly purge ourselves, cleanse our past and unearth some buried treasure that empowers us in the world – and to help others to do so, too.

⚷☊☋ Chiron, the Nodes and the MC

Howard Sasportas (who had Chiron on the MC in Scorpio) once said that this planetoid represented 'the wounds that make us wise', which springs from the well known, myth-based theme of the wounded healer. Chiron asks us to co-habit with the wounds that won't heal but it leaves us the gift of teaching others how to heal their own. Chiron–MC suggests a reputation as a healer, but I've found that some of us with Chiron–MC will (at some point) feel profoundly victimized by the actions of others. Then we must take the ultimate courageous stand to fight a necessary battle. The struggle may include challenging authorities, the community or even our own family in order to maintain our reputation. Our name may suffer from the experience but a moral victory such as this is essential to our healing process. What comes out of it – our gift – is our ability to play mentor to those in similar predicaments.

Whether or not you see the Nodes as having spiritual significance in the chart, when they are conjunct the MC–IC axis (at either end), they nevertheless emphasize the importance of a journey inspired by the themes suggested by the signs on the axis. The lining up of both axes is often found when there's a lifelong obligation to act as parent or mentor to our community. When the North Node is conjunct the IC, the wisest way to proceed is to revisit and plough the past for its wisdom; then we can begin to share our mined gems with the outside world.

It is my hope that this small volume has proven both useful and entertaining to you. In signing off, I leave you with these two engaging quotes:

For life is action – action in any direction. Vibrations are like waves that rise and fall. The wave travels in a definite direction as towards a goal and yet in its movement rises and falls to crest and trough. So people rise and fall, have apparent successes and failures, but all the time may be moving towards their true destination without even knowing it. It is only the one who does not move who does not arrive
– Samuel Lewis, student of Inayat Khan

He has achieved success who has lived well, laughed often and loved much; who has gained the respect of intelligent men and the love of little children; who has filled his niche and accomplished his task; who has left the world better than he found it, whether by an improved poppy, a perfect poem, or a rescued soul; who has never lacked appreciation of earth's beauty or failed to express it; who has always looked for the best in others and given them the best he had; whose life was an inspiration; whose memory a benediction
– Bessie Stanley

Made in the USA
Middletown, DE
23 February 2021